We're On the Move Now!

Cycle B Sermons Based on Second Lessons for Advent, Christmas, and Epiphany

Ronald Love

CSS Publishing Company, Inc.
Lima, Ohio

WE'RE ON THE MOVE NOW!

FIRST EDITION
Copyright © 2020
by CSS Publishing Co., Inc.

The original purchaser may print and photocopy material in this publication for use as it was intended (worship material for worship use; educational material for classroom use; dramatic material for staging or production). No additional permission is required from the publisher for such copying by the original purchaser only. Inquiries should be addressed to: Permissions, CSS Publishing Company, Inc., 5450 N. Dixie Highway, Lima, Ohio 45807.

Library of Congress Cataloging-in-Publication Data:

Names: Love, Ronald H., author. Title: We are on the move! : Cycle B sermons based on second lessons for Advent, Christmas, and Epiphany / Ronald Love. Description: FIRST EDITION. | Lima, Peru : CSS Publishing Company, Inc., 2020. | Identifiers: LCCN 2020015238 | ISBN 9780788030031 (paperback) | ISBN 9780788030048 (ebook) Subjects: LCSH: Bible. New Testament--Sermons. | Common lectionary (1992). Year B. | Advent sermons. | Christmas sermons. | Epiphany--Sermons. Classification: LCC BS2341.55 .L68 2020 | DDC 252/.61--dc23
LC record available at https://lccn.loc.gov/2020015238

For more information about CSS Publishing Company resources, visit our website at www.csspub.com, email us at csr@csspub.com, or call (800) 241-4056.

e-book:
ISBN-13: 978-0-7880-3004-8
ISBN-10: 0-7880-3004-3

ISBN-13: 978-0-7880-3003-1
ISBN-10: 0-7880-3003-5

DIGITALLY PRINTED

To my pastor Chris, who with love and support has truly shepherded me through the perplexities associated of living with Asperger's.

Contents

Preface   7

I Have Been Gifted!   11
Advent 1
1 Corinthians 1:3-9

The Window Of Time Is Closing   16
Advent 2
2 Peter 3:8-15a

Be Near, Ye Faithful   20
Advent 3
1 Thessalonians 5:16-24

We Have All Become Nicodemus   24
Advent 4
Romans 16:25-27

Living In The "In Between" Time   29
Nativity of the Lord
Titus 2:11-14

This Is The End – For Me The Beginning Of Life   34
Christmas 1
Galatians 4:4-7

153 The Abounding Grace Of God   39
Christmas 2
Ephesians 1:3-14

Tata Jesus Is Bangala!   44
Baptism of Our Lord
Acts 19:1-7

Your Body Is A Temple   48
Epiphany 2
1 Corinthians 6:12-20

We're On The Move Now!   53
Epiphany 3
1 Corinthians 7:29-31

A Child Of God   58
Epiphany 4
1 Corinthians 8:1-13

Here I Am, Lord   63
Epiphany 5
1 Corinthians 9:16-23

Into The Valley of Despair   67
Tranfiguration of the Lord
Mark 9:2-9

Preface

A minister has many roles to fulfill in the church. One professor I studied under listed them as three: king, prophet, and priest. In the role of a king you are to administer the church. In the role of a prophet you are to speak to the social issues that are confronting society. In the role of a priest you are to meet the spiritual needs of your congregation.

The United Methodist Church confesses that a minister is called to word, sacrament, and order. The pastor appointed to a local church is to be responsible for the word of God, both in preaching and teaching. A part of this responsibility is that the word of God is an orthodox expression of the scriptures. Regarding the sacrament, only the pastor is permitted to administer the sacraments. This function of his or her office is to protect the sacredness of baptism and holy communion. A pastor's responsibility in maintaining the order of the church is to be certain that all administrative actions of the church are in compliance with the Book of Discipline.

The apostle Paul never clearly defined the role of a minister, but he did give some insight. The church has various offices when he wrote that some are called to be apostles, prophets, evangelists, pastors, and teachers. It should be understood that a minister will ascribed to each of these roles. Though Paul makes it clear that as all Christians are members of the body of Christ, so each has a role to play, it must be realized that the minister is still the one who must oversee and coordinated that organizational structure of the church.

In all the roles outlined as the duty of the pastor, what remains paramount in the minds of parishioners is the ability to preach. As important as being a good administrator is and the comfort that a sincere pastor can bestow, a minister still seems to be judged by his or her ability to preach above all else. This may not be a fair assessment and it may be unfair for those who are great pastors but lack being dynamic preachers, but it is the reality that clergy must deal with.

The apostle Paul did highlight the importance of preaching when he wrote, "How, then, can they call on the one they have not believed in? How can they believe in the one of whom they have not heard? And how can they hear without someone preaching to them?" We can think of preaching as individual witnessing, but the thrust of this message from Paul is to be actually standing before a congregation and proclaiming the good news of Jesus Christ. It is sharing the gospel message of repentance, forgiveness, and salvation. It is sharing the gospel message of the hope and assurance that we have from believing in Jesus. It is the gospel message that articulates that a Christian is kind, gentle, caring, and compassionate. A single sermon may not contain all of these elements, but in the course of the Christian year each of these topics must be highlighted.

The apostle Paul went on to write, "And how can anyone preach unless they are sent? As it is written: 'How beautiful are the feet of those who bring good news!'" If we are called and then sent to preach the good news, then we must take that mandate seriously. This means that sermon preparation cannot be a Saturday night message that is hastily scratched on a dinner table napkin; but, it must be a composition that is carefully crafted days, weeks, and even months in advance of its delivery.

In developing my sermons, I use what I call the 5Es as an outline for sermon preparation and delivery. The 5Es are as follows:

> E = Enlighten: The sermon must spiritually enrich the congregation. The sermon must present the scriptures and theology in a format that is easily comprehended and applied. It must be felt by the congregation that through the presentation they are being drawn closer to God and have a better understanding of themselves and the meaning and purpose of life. Individuals will stop attending a sermon that leaves one despondent as opposed to being lifted up to the throne of God.

> E = Educate: The congregation must feel that they have learned something new from the sermon. They must feel the personal investment of their time was profitable for the information received gave them a better understanding of complementary academic disciplines and life events.

> E = Entertain: The presentation must be interesting and enjoyable to listen to. The attention of the congregation must be maintained or

communication ceases. The mind of bored recipients will drift and eventually be lost altogether. Entertaining is not devoid of meaning, because it is an integral aspect of understanding. Illustrations function as the stained-glass windows in a church sanctuary. Windows of clear glass bring the light of the message that is unfiltered and blinding. A message that is that is seen through stained-glass takes on soft and beautiful hues. A sermon that is blended in the color of stained-glass, rather than being a blinding diatribe through unfiltered clear glass, would enhance the sermon's meaning and promotes its ability to be both listened to and understood. A sermon must have meaningful illustrations to foster comprehension and maintain the attention of the congregation.

E = Enthusiasm: The preacher must be excited about the material and this joy must be conveyed to the congregation. The preacher must be animated, displaying how important the topic under discussion is for him or her. The excitement of the congregation cannot rise above that of the presenter. Enthusiasm underscores that the message is relevant and important, and the preacher desires the audience to share in his or her excitement. Enthusiasm is contagious. If the parishioners who are listening to the discourse and are not enthralled, then they will not remain engaged and feel that the topic is insignificant for their daily living.

E = Encourage: The sermon must challenge the congregation to action. The message must encourage the congregation to become intentional in their endeavors in implementing the sermon's call for action. It is imperative that the congregation is able to apply the message to their current life situation.

Every minister has his or her own style for sermon preparation. Though there are many factors that contribute to that process, the overriding factor is that a pastor develops a method that suits his or her personality. Therefore, I offer my 5Es only as a way for the reader to reexamine his or her present style of sermon preparation, and adopt and adapt any aspect that I present as it compliments your individual personality.

I want to thank you for taking the time to read the sermons in this book, "*We On The Move Now!*" It is my prayer and my hope that the sermons are profitable for your use.

Dr. Ronald H. Love
Florence, South Carolina

Advent 1

1 Corinthians 1:3-9

I Have Been Gifted!

In December 2019, Grace Fellowship United Methodist Church voted to leave its affiliation with the United Methodist Church and partner with the Free Methodist Church. For several years the controversy surrounding the religious issues dealing with the status of homosexuals in the congregation has severely damaged the denomination. A number of individuals have become outspoken activists, promoting varying positions on this dispute. This has consumed a considerable amount of time, energy, and money of the UMC. One result of this theological upheaval is that pastors are performing homosexual marriages, in violation of church doctrine. Because of this, a number of pastors are being put on trial for performing homosexual marriages. This trend has become an unstoppable movement.

A rule that will go into effect in January 2020 states that clergy who officiate at same-sex weddings will receive a minimum one-year unpaid suspension, and a second offense would result in their removal from the clergy. At the next General Conference, to be held in Minneapolis in May 2020, the delegates will debate whether the *Book of Discipline*, the book that outlines the doctrines of the denomination, if the language calling homosexuality as "incompatible with Christian teaching" will be removed. But the real issue before the assembly will be, after years of discussions, debates, and special study committees, will the delegates finally vote to divide the UMC into two bodies? One body will affirm LGBTQ, and the other body will continue with the present doctrinal statement that homosexuality is "incompatible with Christian teaching."

Grace Fellowship has voted to leave the UMC because the congregation can no longer focus on ministry and missions in a dysfunctional denomination. Jim Legett, the founding pastor of Grace Fellowship, said the congregation wanted to "remove ourselves from the dysfunctional fighting going on in the United Methodist Church so that we can fully devote our energies to fulfilling the mission and vision that God has given to us." Leggett said this realization finally came

We're On The Move Now!

upon the congregational leaders when, "At one point, we looked up and noticed that we were spending easily 30% of our leadership meeting time discussing the issues of the UMC, and we realized that this was not good stewardship of our time and resources for the kingdom of God."

Grace Fellowship is not the first church to leave the United Methodist Church as they became disillusioned and were weary of being swallowed up in this controversy.

Controversy engulfed the Corinthian church, and it was the intent of Paul's letter to reestablish unity among the parishioners. Unfortunately, all congregations today are in a constant struggle battling disagreements among parishioners.

Corinth was reestablished as a Roman colony in 44 BCE. Because of its geographic location, the colony became a melting pot for a number of different cultures. This created competition in the market place for ideas, and even physical prowess.

About the year 50 AD, toward the end of Paul's second missionary journey, he established the church in Corinth. With the absence of Paul, as he continued his missionary journey elsewhere, it did not take long for discension and debate to break out among the Christian congregations. There were problems with Christians suing one another in court. There was a dispute over how to administer the sacraments. Sexual immorality appeared to be unceasing. There was the question of what should be the role of women in the church. The disputes caused parishioners to become enraged, and this was coupled with an unwillingness to compromise that the church was splitting into factions. Paul, in his letter, wanted to restore unity and have the Corinthian Christians remember what he taught them.

But before he tackled these issues, he began his letter with words of grace and peace. Paul opened his letter complimenting the Corinthians for the spiritual gifts that God has bestowed upon them. Each and every Corinthian Christian remains unknown to us, but how they each used their spiritual gifts will forever be with us.

We all have been blest with a spiritual gift from God. We often fail to realize that gift. At times we don't feel we are good enough of a person for that special gift. Worse of all is when we fail to use that gift for the betterment of others. Every congregation has tension, ours included, but each congregation is blessed that each person, sitting in the pew before me, has a very special spiritual gift to share with others.

At the age of 87, Dalton Baldwin died on December 12, 2019. His name is unrecognizable to most of us but his name is recognized by some of the greatest soloists across the United States and Europe. For six decades, playing the piano, Baldwin was an accompanist. An accompanist provides the rhythmic or the harmonic support for the melody of a song or instrumental piece. Both in popular music and traditional music, the accompanist provides the beat for the music and outlines the chord progression of the song or instrumental piece.

Baldwin enjoyed most being an accompanist for singers. He once said, "I worship the human voice. There's nothing like singing; it's a romance when you share the music and the poem. The voice is God's instrument." Yet, when Baldwin would be complimented as being the most prominent accompanist in his field, far superior to any other accompanist, he would always reply that he preferred to be simply called a "pianist." Baldwin knew he was good, but humility took precedence over accolades.

This is why Paul could open his letter with these words, "I always thank my God for you because of his grace given you in Christ Jesus. For in him you have been enriched in every way — with all kinds of speech and with all knowledge — God thus confirming our testimony about Christ among you. Therefore, you do not lack any spiritual gift..." Paul is saying that within that dysfunctional community, the Holy Spirit is present. Paul is saying that within that dysfunctional community, every Christian possesses a spiritual gift that can edify the community. With these gifts, the church community should be working in tandem as one body and avoid being recognized as a dysfunctional community that is defined by its disputes.

Paul, in his letters to the various congregations, continually expressed his desire for the believers to continue to grow in their faith and display harmony and unity among the members. For this reason, Paul would often list the spiritual gifts that would enable the congregations to move forward. These spiritual gifts will empower a Christian to live a life of the spirit, and not one of the flesh.

Later in this letter, in the twelfth chapter, Paul listed the spiritual gifts as: administration, apostle, discernment, faith, healing, knowledge, miracles, prophecy, teaching, speaking in tongues, interpretation of tongues and wisdom. But what is important for us, sitting in twenty-first-century pews, is Paul introduced this list with this observation, "There are different kinds of gifts, but the same Spirit distributes them. There are different kinds of service, but the same Lord. There are different kinds of working, but in all of them and in everyone it is the same God at work."

We're On The Move Now!

Because of Paul's introductory statement, I personally understand that spiritual gifts are not limited to speaking in tongues, healing, or being able to perform miracles. I have six academic degrees and a personal library that I built behind my home that contains over 20,000 volumes. I have always considered my spiritual gift to be reading, researching, and writing, which is, since I have Asperger's that is on the autism spectrum, one of my best attributes is how I spend most of my day, to the extent that I don't even own a television set.

We often hear someone say, "I have been gifted." The *Free Dictionary.com* defines gifted as being "endowed with great natural ability, intelligence, or talent: a gifted child; a gifted pianist." People often admire me for my education and the "doctor" that appears before my name. But that is as far as my gift goes. Beyond changing a light bulb, I am a hopeless case at home repair. My knowledge of an automobile is so limited that the most I know is when the warning light goes on take is to take my jeep to a professional mechanic. And anyone who works at a bank shudders when I walk in, as my knowledge of financing is so little, and even after it was patiently explained, I still walk away confused.

With my degrees I reside in the ivory tower of academia. But when I take the time to look up from one of my books, and walk over and look out the window, I see truly gifted men and women whose gifts and skills far exceed my own. I see people doing things that I could never do, such as repairing an automobile, laying bricks, painting a house, fixing an electric transformer, cooking, or stitching up a wound. The list of those gifted talented people, who are able to do that which I could never do, is endless.

Acknowledge your gift. Use your gift for the benefit of others and to the glory of the God who has "gifted" you. People may not long remember your name. They may never know your name. But your gift to them will last forever.

In the 1970s the cost of groceries was soaring upward. Grocery stores are labor-intensive. It means stocking the shelves, placing price tags on all the items, and the time it takes to use a cash register to enter every item that is being purchased is labor intensive. George Lauer, a name I am sure none of you recognize, was concerned about the rising cost of groceries. As an electrical engineer for IBM, working at North Carolina's Research Triangle Park, he set out to find a solution. He eventually developed what is known as the Universal Product Code. We know it better as the tag or label on a product that has a black bar that is configured in black lines with a 12-digit number printed below it. The bar code allows the cashier to simply scan the item being purchased, instead of typing the cost into a cash register. The bar code is faster. It allows for fewer errors, and it allowed the merchant to keep a more accurate inventory. On the twenty-fifth anniversary of his invention Laurer said, "When I watch these clerks zipping the stuff across the scanners and I keep thinking to myself… It can't work that well." We may ask who is George Laurer? And who would know? But we have been forever blessed by this unknown man and his gift to the public.

We have all been gifted. Let us use these gifts to the glory God and to the benefit others.

Amen.

Advent 2

2 Peter 3:8-15a

The Window Of Time Is Closing

Jane Goodall is best known to the world as the foremost expert on chimpanzees. She began her study of chimpanzees in 1960, when she was 23-years-old. She spent the next 55 years studying wild chimpanzees social and family interactions. At the age of 78, she retired from her work as a primatologist and an anthropologist.

Her new venture in life has become being an activist for climate change. Her mother taught her that the best way to change the minds of individuals is to tell stories. Goodall now travels across the globe telling stories of what she has seen of the destruction caused by climate change. She maintains that the only way to stop this devastation is for everyone to get involved. Goodall said in the interview, "My job now is to try and help people understand every one of us makes a difference. And cumulatively, wise choices in how we act each day can begin to change the world."

To make her point clearer, she enjoys telling this story: "I mean, there was a little boy in Burundi. He was seven — a little African boy. I talked at his school. He came up to me afterward, and he said, 'If I pick up a piece of litter every day, I'll make a difference, won't I?' I said, 'Yes. You'll make a huge difference.' And I said, 'Well, suppose you persuade ten of your friends to do the same?' He said, 'Wow. That would really make a difference.' And I said, 'Then each of your ten friends could choose ten friends.' He said, 'Hoo — we'd change everything.'"

Goodall has a new goal. A serious goal. A goal that motivates her. That goal is to convince people and nations that climate change is real and appropriate steps must be taken to stop it. Of her new role as an activist Goodall said, "I'm traveling around the world now, no longer studying chimpanzees, and trying to tell people what's happening in the world, the mess that we've made and the fact that unless we all get together to help the environment we all share, then it may be too late. The window of time is closing. And it's not enough just to wave placards and say, 'Climate change!' The point is to take actual action. To do your bit."

Advent 2

The window of time is closing.

The message of 2 Peter is that the window of time for the second coming is quickly closing.

There is a scholarly debate if Peter is the actual author of the letter, but it is sufficient for us to claim Peter as the author. This question brings forth another question, and that would be the year in which the letter was written. Peter was executed by the Romans in the year 68, and it is believed that he wrote this letter shortly before that.

One of the most often quoted lines from the Bible is when Peter wrote: "But do not forget this one thing, dear friends: With the Lord a day is like a thousand years, and a thousand years are like a day." We often associate this line with unanswered prayers, a delayed healing, asking why I can't find someone to marry, or when will God rescue me from my plight. This is just a very short list of how we have used this verse when God seems unresponsive in our lives. And, perhaps, this is a meaningful interpretation.

Though, for Peter, in the five preceding verses, informs us of his meaning for composing a standard of time for God. Peter wrote, "Above all, you must understand that in the last days scoffers will come, scoffing and following their own evil desires. They will say, 'Where is this 'coming' he promised? Ever since our ancestors died, everything goes on as it has since the beginning of creation.' But they deliberately forget that long ago by God's word, the heavens came into being and the earth was formed out of water and by water. By these waters also the world of that time was deluged and destroyed. By the same word the present heavens and earth are reserved for fire, being kept for the day of judgment and destruction of the ungodly."

Peter is saying that God is delaying the second coming desiring that as many who are willing to be saved are saved. The "slowness" will allow unbelievers to turn from their secular ways and live spiritual lives. It is the hope that they will no longer live in darkness but will come and live in the great light. The line expresses the hope that everyone will invite Jesus into their lives as Lord and Savior.

Unbelievers denied the second coming. They argued that this was a stable world in which things, since the of Jesus' death on a cross, have remained unalterably the same. They believed since God was so slow to act that it was possible to assume that the second coming was never going to happen at all. They had no desire to change from their debauchery lifestyle.

But Peter disputes this line of thinking when he wrote, "The Lord is not slow in keeping his promise, as some understand slowness. Instead he is patient with you, not wanting anyone to perish, but everyone to come to repentance. But the day of the Lord will come like a thief. The heavens will disappear with a roar; the elements will be destroyed by fire, and the earth and everything done in it will be laid bare." God's slowness is not a declaration that there is no God, but God's slowness is an act of mercy hoping everyone will come to believe.

Jesus anticipated this problem among unbelievers when he said, "As it was in the days of Noah, so it will be at the coming of the Son of Man. For in the days before the flood, people were eating and drinking, marrying and giving in marriage, up to the day Noah entered the ark; and they knew nothing about what would happen until the flood came and took them all away. That is how it will be at the coming of the Son of Man."

The seriousness of what Jesus spoke, and Peter wrote, should compel us to be evangelists because the window is closing.

We don't have the privilege of waiting until tomorrow. We must act this day. This hour. This minute. We need to share our testimony and why we came to believe in Jesus Christ as our Lord and Savior. We must encourage individuals to invite Jesus into their lives. We must be willing to share biblical passages. We need to avoid excuse making as to why I am not qualified to be an evangelist. We need to stop pretending that we don't know anyone who is not already a Christian. And as much as I dislike scare tactics, we must be serious in our presentation that there is a day of judgment.

Lauren Daigle is a Christian singer who has won most every award possible for her inspiring songs. A part of her evangelical mission is preforming concerts at state penitentiaries. In December 2019, she performed at the Angola State Penitentiary in Louisiana. Angola is the largest maximum-security facility in the United States. Between songs Daigle offered encouraging words to the inmates. It was her desire to help them find a new direction in life. She hoped her songs and her performance would lead some of the inmates to Christ. For those who would not accept Jesus as their Savior, she hoped her songs would offer comfort.

Between one song Daigle said, "He doesn't point a finger, he doesn't give you shame, He sits with you. I think that's why he's called the Savior of the world." To date her most popular album, which was released in September 2018, is *Look Up Child*. During her performance of songs from that album, she paused and said to the inmates, "The one thing that you can always do is look up. You can look up and see the sky. You can look up and see the kindness of God, and his extravagant love for each one of you." In the song she sings when your world is in "darkness," when your world is "crumbling," you should, as she sings in the refrain, "Look up child."

Amen.

Advent 3

1 Thessalonians 5:16-24

Be Near, Ye Faithful

The origin of this well-known Christmas carol *O Come, All Ye Faithful* remains a mystery. For several hundred years it was maintained that it was written by a cleric in the Middle Ages. The earliest known manuscript of the hymn was discovered 1740. The discovery of the manuscript is attributed to John Francis Wade. In England he was a copyist and writer of church music. At this time there was a Holy War between the Church of England and the Roman Catholic Church. Ward, in 1745, left England and took up residence in Douay, France. Several years later he was ordained as a Catholic priest. Ward was a calligrapher by training, and a skilled musician. These talents allowed Ward make copies of the hymn and distribute the sheet music across Europe. The tune name *Adeste Fideles* came from the first words of the hymn in Latin, meaning "Be near, ye faithful."

Frederick Oakley translated the hymn from Latin, which began with the familiar line "O come, all ye faithful." The hymn was first published in 1852 in F. H. Murray's *Hymnal for Use in the English Church*.

The hymn, now in the public domain, is an invitation to "come, all ye faithful," which places the singer among the faithful shepherds who rushed to see the Christ child:

O come, all ye faithful,
Joyful and triumphant!
O come ye, O come ye to Bethlehem;
Come and behold him
Born the King of Angels:

The shepherds then went forth to tell others. This is reflected in the verse:

O Sing, choirs of angels,
Sing in exultation,
Sing all that hear in heaven God's holy word.

Advent 3

Years after the Bethlehem event, the leaders of the first century church went to the manger in spirit and saw the Son of God. They then felt duty bound, as the shepherds did, to share this good news with everyone.

The leaders of the first-century church believed in immediate return of Christ. They held so strongly to this belief that they expected to see in their lifetime the return of Christ on the clouds of heaven. This is certainly the belief that was held by Paul, and it influenced much of his teaching. For instance, a letter from Paul arrived at the church in Corinth with these words, "Now to the unmarried and the widows I say: It is good for them to stay unmarried, as I do. But if they cannot control themselves, they should marry, for it is better to marry than to burn with passion." We need to understand that Paul was not opposed to marriage, he just thought that it was unnecessary with the immediate return of Christ. He just felt that the time devoted to a spouse would be better spent serving the evangelical mission of the church.

The Roman Catholic Church today still maintains the tradition of celibacy. A celebrate priest is married to the church, as such a spouse will not interfere with his pastoral work. Pope Francis also maintains that celibacy is a tradition of the church. The foundation for this tradition is that the twelve apostles were all celibate men. Francis believes that celibacy is only a tradition of the church, which prevents married men to become priests. He did note that celibacy should not be eliminated globally, but culturally. The pope did make it clear that celibacy is not a doctrine of the church, but a tradition of the church. It is a discipline that priests accept. Because of this there are cultural situations where a priest can marry.

This is especially true in cultural regions where there is a severe shortage of priests. Francis said, "There is, actually, nothing new here. The archbishop is correct in stating that clerical celibacy is not a dogma. It is a matter of discipline and — although I have yet to see a mainstream media story point this out — there are, in fact, married priests today, even in the Latin rite of the Catholic church, where most priests are required to be celibate."

With the immediate return of Christ on the horizon, Paul calls, "O come all ye faithful" to remain spiritually disciplined until Christ is seen on the clouds of heaven. Paul then offers advice on how to remain spiritually disciplined and pure in heart while waiting for the return of Christ.

In our lectionary reading, Paul lists what a disciplined Christian must do to remain spiritually strong while waiting for the *parousia*, which means the day of judgment. We are not expected to go to the extreme of celibacy, which is an acceptable path for those who choose it, but we must heed the instructions provided by the apostle Paul. The Christian should be one that is always giving thanks, even in the harshest situations. The Christian must be receptive to the guidance of the Holy Spirit. The Christian must be attentive to the prophets. The Christian must be respectful and obedient to their leaders. The Christian must have the spiritual strength and discipline to "hold on to what is good, reject every kind of evil."

Being spiritual does not come naturally, but it must be nurtured. It requires that we are focused on being spiritual. It requires self-examination, questioning ourselves if we are living examples of Jesus. In a secular world it is so easy to live by the flesh, so we must constantly avoid places and people who will tempt us. It means we forsake Satan, and we are always on guard to protect ourselves from Satan's deceitful ways. It means we no longer walk in darkness; it means we don't even have the inclination to walk in darkness. We only want to be individuals whose sole desire is to walk in the light. Paul calls us to always have the mindset of worship, or as a stanza from our hymn reads, "O come, let us adore him, Christ the Lord."

Even though this is the twenty-first-century, we cannot dismiss Satan as a real demonic power whose intention is to separate us from Christ. Paul, with a strong belief in evil spirits, was concerned that Christians remain faithful to God until the second coming.

Martin Luther is considered the father of the Protestant Reformation. This is when a significant number of Christians left Roman Catholicism, most of whom resided in Germany. Luther, as the leader of the movement, was excommunicated by Pope Leo X. After his excommunication, as ordered by the pope, Luther appeared before the Diet of Worms on April 18, 1521. Before the gathered hierarchy of the Catholic church, Luther still refused to recant. At the conclusion of the assembly Pope Leo X declared Luther an outlaw. With this declaration the pope ordered that it is a crime for anyone in Germany to give Luther food or shelter. It permitted anyone to kill Luther without legal consequence.

When Luther left the summit, Frederick the Wise had him kidnapped and taken to Wartburg Castle for his protection. There Luther would be safe from the Court of Inquisition and those who sought his life. While residing in the safety of the castle, Luther translated the Bible from Greek into German, the native tongue Saxony. It was now possible for the laity to read the Bible for themselves.

It was also here that Satan continually attacked Luther, trying to prevent him from completing his translation of the Bible. It is here that we have the famous story that Luther finally became so angry at Satan that he threw his inkwell at him. If you would visit the castle, even today you can see the ink stain on the castle wall.

Paul offered his ideas on how to remain spiritually alive so Christians don't succumb to these evil spirits. We accomplish this by engaging in spiritual disciplines. We attend Sunday school, and then we go to the sanctuary to worship. We are involved in the Bible studies, small groups, and fellowship gatherings that the church offers. We also realize that we have a personal responsibility to have private devotions each day at home.

John Bunyan was a Puritan pastor, who is best known to us for his book *Pilgrim's Progress*. He preached his last sermon at Mr. Gamman's meeting-house, near Whitechapel in England, on August 19, 1688. Twelve days after preaching this sermon John Bunyan died. The text for the sermon was John 1:13. The message of the sermon is that every man and woman must examine themselves in order to know if they are born again or not. In his last sermon, Bunyan described the signs of a new birth. In the sermon, Bunyan asked his listeners, "Are you brought out of the dark dungeon of this world into Christ?" He went on to say that an individual "cannot you be quiet without you have a bellyful of the milk of God's word?" He went on to say, "When we see a king's son play with a beggar, this is unbecoming; so if you be the king's children, live like the king's children; if you be risen with Christ, set your affections on things above, and not on things below…"

As we await the *parousia*, let us "Be near, ye faithful."

Amen.

Advent 4

Romans 16:25-27

We Have All Become Nicodemus

John Wycliffe is best known to us as a Bible translator. He is remembered as a historical figure for translating the Vulgate, the Bible written in Latin that only the priests could read, into English, a Bible which the common man could read for himself. We also recognize him from the organization that was established in his name, the Wycliffe Bible Translators. It is the mission of this organization to translate the Bible into the common vernacular of every country that presently does not have a Bible that can be read by the general populace.

Wycliffe was a part of the Protestant Reformation that rejected many of the theological positions and practices of the Roman Catholic Church. This led to his dismissal as a professor at Oxford University in 1381. In 1384 he died of a stroke and was buried.

The Catholic church continued to view Wycliffe as a heretic because of his challenges to the doctrines of Roman Catholicism. Condemned as a heretic, at the Council of Constance in 1415, Pope Martin V ordered that Wycliffe's body be exhumed and burned, the same punishment for all heretics.

But this was not the end of Wycliffe's story. The townspeople came to Lutterworth and took his ashes and deposited them into the river. The ashes then floated from Lutterworth to the Avon, and from the Avon into the Severn, and from the Severn into the ocean. The ashes of Wycliffe became an emblem of his doctrine which was now dispersed the world over.

We are to preach the word of God so it will be spread across the globe. This is the message that Paul presents to us in the closing paragraph of the book of Romans. Paul begins by telling us that God's message has become a part of our lives. Then Paul concludes that since God's message was so life-changing for each and every one of us, that we are to share God's message with others.

Paul wrote in the opening line of his summary statement to his letter to the churches in Rome, "Now to God who is able to establish you in accordance with my gospel, the message I proclaim about Jesus Christ." Paul wrote that we have consumed the word of God, and it has changed our lives. The word of God has become a part of our being. With these words, in the closing paragraph in what biblical scholars consider Romans to be the outline of Paul's systematic theology, he concludes in his closing that the word of God has engulfed our lives. Paul confesses that the word of God dwells within us.

This, certainly, has changed us. To use some biblical imagery we are the shepherds of the flock, not hirelings; we no longer live in darkness, but have come into the light; we no longer live by the flesh, but we now live by the spirit; we are no longer the sons of predation, but we are the children of God; we no longer live a life of judging others, but we now live a life that understands forgiveness; we are no longer guided by hate, but we now are motivated by compassion; we are no longer self-centered, but we understand the meaning of humility. We have replaced ridicule with grace.

We have all become Nicodemus. Nicodemus was a Pharisee, the legalistic Jewish sect that was adamantly opposed to Jesus. It was the leaders of the Pharisees who stirred up the crowd, as Jesus stood before them next to Pontius Pilate, to yell, "Crucify him! Crucify him!" Nicodemus, knowing he would lose his status in society if he was seen with Jesus, so he came to Jesus unseen in the night. Nicodemus was also held in high regard because he was a member of the Sanhedrin, the ruling assembly that presided over the Jews. Another reason to come unseen in the darkness of night.

Nicodemus was aware of the teachings of Jesus and wanted to know for himself if this is how we are to live. In response to Nicodemus inquiry Jesus replied, "Very truly I tell you, no one can see the kingdom of God unless they are born again." Confused, Nicodemus asked, "How can someone be born when they are old? Surely they cannot enter a second time into their mother's womb to be born!" The scriptures go on to report Jesus' answer to Nicodemus, "Very truly I tell you, no one can enter the kingdom of God unless they are born of water and the Spirit. Flesh gives birth to flesh, but the Spirit gives birth to spirit." It is from this incident in the life of Jesus we have come to hear the common phrase that a Christian is "born again."

We were born into original sin. We have now been "born again" into the life of Jesus.

The television actor Tom Selleck said he owes his success because of his faith in Jesus. Selleck confessed that Jesus has guided him over the years. After college, Selleck planned to have a career with United Airlines. He caught the attention of Hollywood from the television commercials that he was doing while working for United, and from these commercials he was even offered an acting contract by Twentieth Century Fox. He turned it down believing that God had called him to serve in the army. After serving in the army, Selleck returned to Hollywood to pursue an acting career.

His big break came when he was offered the lead role in the television series *Magnum, P.I.* The show ran from 1980 to 1988. In a December 2019 interview with *CBN News*, Selleck said, "A man's heart plans his way, but the Lord directs his steps. Humble yourselves, therefore, under God's mighty hand, that he may lift you up in due time." Regarding the fame and fortune that acting has brought to him, Selleck confesses that his relationship with Jesus has kept him grounded. The actor said, "I try very hard to conduct myself in an ethical way, because that's important to my stability now. We're a culture that's so centered on the individual. The culture says that basically nothing is more important than the way you feel."

Paul in his concluding statement to the churches in Rome articulated that when we accept Jesus into our lives — when we are born gain — that we become renewed individuals who live in the image of Jesus. Paul then went on to instruct the Christians in Rome, and all the Christians he encountered on his missionary journeys, and in the timeless nature of the Bible to us today, that we are to share that good news with others. We are to be evangelists.

Paul wrote in his concluding paragraph to his letter, "but now revealed and made known through the prophetic writings by the command of the eternal God, so that all the Gentiles might come to the obedience that comes from faith — to the only wise God be glory forever through Jesus Christ! Amen."

It was originally understood by the first followers of Jesus that he came just for the Jews. Jesus was the long expected Jewish Messiah spoken of by the prophets. A few years later, as Paul began his missionary journeys, he held to the doctrine that Jesus was the Messiah for all people. Jesus came for the Jews and the non-Jews alike, which would be the Gentiles.

The word "Gentile" means all nations except the nation of Israel. In course of time, as the Jews began to more and more to pride themselves on their peculiar privileges as the "chosen ones," the word Jew acquired unpleasant associations, and was often used as a term of contempt. Paul,

Advent 4

disagreeing with this ideology, saw his mission to be one to the Jews and Gentiles, that is, to all the citizens of the world. He understood that Jesus was the Messiah not just for the Jews, but for all individuals of any ethnic and cultural background. Rome, being a cosmopolitan city, had a very diverse population. Paul realized that the message of Jesus was for all the citizens of Rome; it was likewise the message for all the citizens of the world.

Of our many responsibilities as Christians, one of the foremost is to be an evangelist. And not far from where you are sitting in the pew there is a massive missionary field. We probably realize it; we just won't acknowledge it.

There are many reasons why we don't assume the role of being an evangelist. And the list of reasons is common to us all, as we have heard them so often and even used them ourselves. Probably the two most common are: "I don't know the Bible well enough to answer someone's questions." And the other being, "Everyone I know is a Christian." Feeling unqualified and unnecessary, we forsake the task of being an evangelist.

We also realize, if we are willing to admit it, that we do know enough. We also realize, if we are willing to admit it, that even though one professes to be a Christian they may have never really dedicated themselves to the teachings of Jesus.

You are qualified because you believe. You don't need to know all the answers, you only need to know how to express, with sincerity, what Jesus means to you. As for not knowing anyone who is not a Christian, that is not your place to judge. The only thing you need to know is how to be attentive enough to enter into their lives, at the proper time, with the appropriate message of Jesus.

When we hear the name Carry Nation we immediately associate it with prohibition. She was born as Carrier Amelia Moore in November 1846 in the state of Kentucky. After the Civil War, when she was 21-years-old, her family moved to Missouri. There she married a young doctor, Charles Gloyd. Charles served with the Union in the war, and on his return he was an alcoholic. His alcoholism went to such an extreme that he could no longer support Carry. When Carry became pregnant she left Charles and returned to live with her parents. A few months after her daughter, Charlien — named after her father — was born, Charles died. Carry was able to rebuild her life, becoming a school teacher and marrying a lawyer, David Nation.

Over the years the scar of alcoholism left upon Nation's soul did not leave her soul. She began to have visions and became increasing religious. After David Nation became a pastor, the family moved once again, this time to Kansas. It was in Kansas that Carry Nation organized the local chapter of the Women's Christian Temperance League.

The Women's Christian Temperance Union was founded in 1874, and its goal was to abolish the sale of alcohol because of the suffering it caused to families, specifically to women and children whose husbands and fathers drank to excess. At a time when women lacked legal rights and recourses and had to depend on male breadwinners for some or all of the family income, an alcoholic spouse, and perhaps violent and abusive alcoholic spouse, seriously endangered the household. The anti-alcohol crusade quickly came to also encompass other perceived sources of social "impurity," such as smoking and sexual promiscuity. The union proposed to cure these vices through empowering women to vote and through the social ministrations of middle-class white women.

Nation took a more direct-action approach to the prohibition crusade. On December 27, 1900, she used a hatchet to smash up the bar at the Carey Hotel in Wichita. She was arrested but was released shortly after her incarceration. Though, she now became famous and front-page news as the prohibitionist who carried a hatchet and wrecked a saloon.

Nation, who was almost six feet tall, used her imposing presence to promote her movement and her brand. She also moved outside of Kansas, where the sale of alcohol was already technically illegal, and brought her vision, and her hatchet, to other saloons.

Her behavior provoked a tremendous uproar and sent her to jail repeatedly for disorderly conduct and disturbing the peace. Her fines were paid by the sale of pewter hatchet pins. Nation wielded her voice as effectively as her hatchet, eloquently speaking her mind and inspiring others. She was able to support herself from her speaking fees.

Nation and her husband divorced in 1901. After the divorce she continued, for the rest of her life, her prohibition campaign. The speaking fees she received enabled her to buy a small farm in Arkansas. The purpose of the farm was to turn it into a prohibition school to teach other campaigners. However, she died in January 1911, before the school could be completed and almost a decade before the Eighteenth Amendment was passed.

We are empowered by the word of God that dwells within us. Empowered by God, we are to proclaim the gospel message to others, while acting upon its commands for justice.

Amen.

Nativity of the Lord
Titus 2:11-14

Living In The "In Between" Time

Devon Still had encountered many difficulties in life, some of which were of his own doing. Playing football became his salvation. The six feet-five inch, 310 pound defensive end was drafted by the Cincinnati Bengals in 2012. His lifelong ambition had arrived, but injuries kept him off the field of play for many games. This resulted in playing for the Houston Texans in 2016, and the next year on the practice squad for the New York Jets. After that season, Still was dismissed from professional football.

Still grew up in Wilmington, Delaware. His parents were not churchgoers, and when he was in the fifth grade, his parents divorced. He went to live with his grandmother. It was also the beginning of his acting out and stealing. Grandma began taking Devon to church every Sunday. She had taken him to church before, but this time he knew it was for punishment.

Still said of his spiritual journey, "I'm a person of faith, though there have been times I've felt disconnected from God. Like when injuries threatened to derail my NFL career. I'd remember what my grandma told me when she was dragging me to church as a kid back in Wilmington, 'The Lord speaks to all of us, Devon, but you're never going to hear him if you don't open your ears and listen.'"

Yet, even as an adult, Still could not hear the voice of God. When he prayed, he came to the understanding to never expect an answer, at least not one like my grandma used to hear. To hear grandma tell it, the Almighty talking to her in a booming Old Testament voice, one where there was no mistaking that it was the voice of God. Still feared that he was never going to have that kind of relationship with God. He knew that he owed everything to God; yet, he pondered, was it too much to ask for some actual spoken words from God?

In his junior year at Penn State, Still got a coed pregnant. Into that relationship, daughter Leah was born. The couple tried to work out their relationship, but it did not happen. In the separation, Still promised to always be with Leah.

After college he was drafted by the Cincinnati Bengals. In his second year with the Bengals, Still encountered what was thought to be his football ending injury. In December 2013, playing against the Pittsburgh Steelers, Still strained his back. By that night, he couldn't walk. Again, he needed surgery. The pain was unrelenting. An ultrasound revealed three blood clots in his lungs. The doctor informed him, "You'll never play football again."

It was also during this period in his life that he met Asha. It was a relationship of mutual love and support

Devon asked Asha, "Why does everything keep going wrong?" The huge defensive end was practically in tears. With spiritual insight, Asha replied, "Maybe you need to have a real relationship with God. Not just a help-me-out-of-a-jam one."

Asha and Devon joined a Pentecostal church. Devon was amazed at how hard that congregation prayed. The church welcomed Asha and Devon with open arms. For the first time, Devon understood the importance of a church community — a church team that always has your back. A month after the couple started attending, Still went back to the doctor. The blood clots were gone. Devon said, "All those prayers, said by people who barely knew me. I knew I'd been led there." That April, Asha and Devon were baptized. Finally, Devon felt as if his life had turned a corner.

Then in June 2014, Leah was diagnosed with a mass growing in her abdomen. It was Stage IV neuroblastoma. As Still related his feelings, "Right there in the hospital waiting room, I fell to my knees. I'd never taken a hit that hard playing football. My head was spinning. And I felt a flash of anger. What did God want from me? Then I thought of the people at church, their incredible support. I was going to need them more than ever. But more than ever, I craved that one-on-one connection to God. His voice booming in my ears. As it had for my grandmother."

Still felt closer to God, but he also wondered why God seemed so distant and quiet. Devon said, "it still seemed as if I was doing all the talking. I tried not to take it personally — until Leah, my sweet four-year-old daughter, got sick with cancer. I really needed to hear directly from him then."

After the June 2 diagnosis, Devon spent the next three weeks sleeping beside his daughter at the hospital. In support of his daughter, Still shaved his head bald and said that he would grow his hair back only when Leah did.

Spending so much time at the hospital, Still saw many other parents suffering emotionally for their children. Also, he could not avoid the trauma that the children were experiencing. Still began a campaign to raise awareness and support on his Instagram account. Soon he had a half million followers.

Eventually Still had to retire from football, but he continued his campaign for cancer awareness in young children. Devon Still said, "My entire life God has been talking to me, in ways I just hadn't been hearing."

Still recounts his spiritual life journey in his book, *Still in the Game: Finding the Faith to Tackle Life's Biggest Challenges.*

We listen, and then we proclaim God's power with our own lives.

Paul sent a letter, written between 66 and 67 AD, that was carried by his ambassadors to Titus, who was residing on the island of Crete. Titus was left behind on Crete after Paul left the Mediterranean Island to continue his missionary journey. Paul left Titus to oversee the churches on the island to be sure they were disciplined, ministered to individuals and to appoint congregational leaders who were moral and adhered to the gospel message that Paul taught during his visit. This letter was to encourage the leaders of the church in the absence of the physical presence of Paul.

One of the most significant messages from this morning's lectionary reading is that the Christians on Crete lived in the "in between" times. As it was their message in the first century, it is our message today in the twenty-first century.

Paul wrote about the two great appearances of Jesus Christ. In chapter two, verse eleven, the first appearance of Jesus is recorded. This verse reads, "For the grace of God has appeared that offers salvation to all people." This first appearance was when Jesus walked among us, teaching and healing. The second appearance, which is recorded in chapter two, verse thirteen, was when Jesus will appear again at the *parousia*, the second coming. This verse reads, "While we wait for the blessed hope — the appearing of the glory of our great God and Savior, Jesus Christ..." We are now living in between these two appearances — the incarnation and the second coming.

The challenge of this in-between living is neither be preoccupied with the past or the future, but to live one's life in self-control, anticipating Christ's return. We are to pursue godliness and righteousness while we live in the present.

Those who believed in the first appearance of Jesus listened. Can we today? We can say, as Devon Still did, "My entire life God has been talking to me, in ways I just hadn't been hearing." But now we do hear? We have invited Jesus into our lives. We have been converted. We have been "born again." Being born again, it is our challenge, which requires a great deal of self-discipline, to continue to hear Jesus until we can rejoice in Jesus second appearance. We keep the words of grandma, spoken to her grandson Devon back in Wilmington, "The Lord speaks to all of us, Devon, but you're never going to hear him if you don't open your ears and listen."

Now that we are listening to Jesus, we must live as imitators of Jesus. In a single, recorded verse, verse twelve, Paul clearly stated what that obedient and disciplined life means when he wrote, "It teaches us to say 'No' to ungodliness and worldly passions, and to live self-controlled, upright and godly lives in this present age…" We have to say "no," that we will never live according to the flesh. We have to say "yes," that we will live guided by the Holy Spirit.

Augustine was born in 354 and died in 430. He is often known to us as Augustine of Hippo, as he was made bishop of Hippo Regus in Northern Africa. Augustine was extremely well educated. He was one of the four doctors, which means teachers, of Western Christianity. The other three were Ambrose, Jerome, and Pope Gregory I. Augustine's writings influenced the late fourth-and early fifth-century church, and still guides us to this day. In his commentary on Titus 2:12 Augustine wrote:

> *But there is a great and general fasting, which is perfect fasting, to abstain from the inequities and illicit pleasures of the world: "that, by denying ungodliness and worldly desires, we may live soberly and justly and godly in this world." What reward does the apostle add to this fasting? He continues and says, "Looking for that blessed hope and the manifestation of the glory of the blessed God and Savior, Jesus Christ."*

We are to say "no" to the illicit pleasures of worldly living. We may not want to admit it publicly, but we all have temptations that we fight off daily. We have to accept this as a part of being human. It would not be wrong to say that we are doing battle with Satan, who has a very strong and powerful evil spirit. But now, as we are able to listen to God, we have the spiritual strength to say "no" to the wilily evils of Satan. As Paul wrote the gospels "teaches us to say 'No' to ungodliness and worldly passions…"

But don't only live in a world of "no," we also live in a world of "yes." As Paul indicated that we are not alone in our desire to live godly lives, because supporting us is the presence of Jesus. Paul wrote that the Holy Spirit will teach us, "to live self-controlled, upright, and godly lives in this present age…" And once we discover the joy of living a life in the Spirit, we will have no desire to return to a life lived in the flesh.

So, as his grandma dragged young Devon Still to her Baptist church each and every Sunday, she gave us all words of advice, "The Lord speaks to all of us, Devon, but you're never going to hear him if you don't open your ears and listen."

Amen.

Christmas 1

Galatians 4:4-7

This Is The End — For Me The Beginning Of Life

The chronology of this period of Paul's life is difficult to accurately establish. From my reading and research, I outline it as follows:

The apostle Paul visited Galatia during his second and third missionary journeys. Galatia is in Asia Minor and had become a Roman province under Caesar Augustus in 25 BC. It was originally a small geographic area, but the Romans would often expand a geographical title to the extended lands beyond the original borders. It was Paul's practice to use the Roman provincial titles.

The most important theme in this letter was salvation through faith in Jesus Christ. Paul was particularly concerned with the controversy surrounding the gentile Christians and the Mosaic law. Paul argued that the gentile Galatians did not need to adhere to the tenets of the Mosaic law, particularly the Jewish religious rite of male circumcision. The role of the Mosaic law was replaced by the revelation of Christ.

It was during Paul's first visit to Galatia, that he contracted malaria along the low-lying coastlands. Seeking to regain his health, Paul move inward to the highlands of the interior. It was here that Paul discovered a number of synagogues that had been established. The pagans, the predominant belief system in the area, associated themselves with a synagogue became known as "Jewish proselytes," which we now refer to as "Jewish Christians." The problem that these new Jewish Christians experienced was the expectation that they continue to obey Jewish law and follow Jewish customs. Those who were most adamant in enforcing this doctrine were known as "Judaizers." The word *Judaizer* comes from a Greek verb meaning "to live according to Jewish customs." Judaizers were former Jews who now professed being a Christian but still taught that it was necessary to adopt Jewish customs and practices, especially those found in the law of Moses.

When Paul returned to Galatia for the second time, he was appalled that little had changed and perhaps things had gotten worse. The

Judaizers were still prying upon the infant, or newest, Christians. It was an unrelenting propaganda attack in an attempt to make them Jewish Christians. The pagans, the gentiles, who were so willing to convert to Christianity, were now turning back to their former ways of worshipping idols. Some had left the church altogether, others were bringing their heathen practices into the church, influencing its worship and doctrines. Paul did what he could to alleviate the situation, but he made little progress.

After Paul left Galatia, he continued to get news of the unsavory conditions the Galatian churches were in and how the Christians, who were both former Jews and pagan gentiles, were becoming agnostics. This inspired Paul to write, from Corinth where he was presently residing, his letter to the churches in Galatia.

In all of Paul's letters, in our lectionary reading for today, we have most forthright and boldest declaration of the "incarnation" that the apostle Paul ever made. Paul wrote, "God sent his Son, born of a woman..." With this confession, Paul affirms one of the earliest first-century doctrines of the church, and that is, Jesus is God. Though this doctrine is so easily accepted by us today, from the first century and for the next several centuries that followed, this interpretation was controversial. Yet, despite the many alternative churches that arose with competing doctrines, the belief that Jesus was God always prevailed. It was always the predominant belief.

By becoming fully man Jesus does live within us, and we live within Jesus. Paul wrote, "born under the law, to redeem those under the law, that we might receive adoption to children." We no longer live under the tyranny of the Mosaic law, as such we have been adopted by God. Therefore, Paul can write, "Because you are his sons, God sent the Spirit of his Son into our hearts, the Spirit who calls out, '*Abba*, Father.'"

In this line Paul preserved the Aramaic word, *Abba*, the language Jesus spoke; and the Greek word, *Father*, the language of the Roman Empire. The word *Abba* is so sacred that the early writers of the scriptures, which would include Paul, never translated it from Aramaic to Greek. In the scriptures, Jesus only spoke the word *Abba* once, and that was the opening words of his prayer in the Garden of Gethsemane, shortly before his execution. Though, some scholars think that Jesus began every prayer with *Abba*. The Lord's Prayer being one of the most noteworthy examples. Using this personal address was one more reason the Pharisees desired to end the influence that Jesus had.

Abba is an intimate word, and it is most often translated as "Daddy."

Having been adopted by God, instead of living under the strict regulations of Jewish law, by grace through Christ we have been redeemed, we have been forgiven, we have been adopted. We are able to address God as *Abba* — our "Daddy."

As children of God we can now place our full trust in God. We can have total confidence in God. We are assured that God will watch over and protect us. This does not mean we will escape all the harsh realities of life, as Jesus experienced in the Garden of Gethsemane, but as Jesus never lost his faith in God, we also find our solace, our comfort, in knowing that the God of creation is also our heavenly Father — our *Abba*.

Out of prison, televangelist Jim Bakker once again has his own Christian talk show. He once presided over the PTL Club, but it went bankrupt as a result of Bakker using it as his personal showcase to gain personal wealth. Bakker and his PTL associates sold $1,000 "lifetime memberships," entitling buyers to an annual three-night stay at a luxury hotel at Heritage USA, located in Charlotte, North Carolina. According to the prosecution at Bakker's fraud trial, tens of thousands of memberships were sold but only one 500-room hotel was ever finished. Bakker sold "exclusive partnerships" that exceeded capacity, raising more than twice the money needed to build the hotel. Some of the money paid Heritage USA's operating expenses and Bakker kept $3.4 million for himself. As a result of this, Bakker was found guilty of 24 counts of fraud and conspiracy. He was sentenced to four years in a federal penitentiary. PTL means "Praise the Lord," but the common joke became that PTL meant "Pass the Loot."

After prison, Bakker went back on television. Bakker has shown no remorse, and in fact has continued in his arrogant ways. Bakker on his show in January 2020 declared that President Trump is the litmus test for salvation. Bakker said, "You know what? Trump is a test whether you're even saved. Only saved people can love Trump."

It is these hypocritical evangelists that sometimes makes us want to hide that we are children of God. But we must always keep before us that it is God himself that has adopted us, so we should never be afraid to share with others that "I am a child of God." Paul, after detailing the incarnation of Jesus, proclaimed that Jesus came "in order to redeem." Trump does carry the nuclear launch codes, known as the Gold Codes, the codes printed on a piece of plastic the size of a bank card that has been nicknamed "the Biscuit," but Trump does not have the power to forgive sins. It is pagan worship to think that the president of the United

States must be loved to be saved. We do not call Trump *Abba*; we call him Mr. President. There is a big difference.

This is why when we find ourselves in the Garden of Gethsemane we are not going to seek help from Jim Bakker or Donald Trump, or for that matter from the self-centered preachers of the prosperity gospel; such as: Joel Osteen, Creflo Dollar, Benny Hinn, TD Jakes, Joyce Meyer, Paula White, Kenneth Copland, Robert Tilton, Eddie Long, Juanita Bynum, or Paul Crouch. These pseudo-pastors will watch over you long enough to inspire you to give money so they can have another Lear jet; but, you won't find them being crucified upside down as Peter was, doing so because he felt unworthy to be crucified right side up as his Lord was. Only someone who knew they were an adopted child of God, as Peter knew, could have such assurance in the God whom he could call *Abba*.

To know that we are a child of God, adopted into his family, should give us all a sense of peace and tranquility. Even during the times when we are anxious, scared, hurting, indecisive, we know that we are always under the protective gaze of God.

Dietrich Bonhoeffer is a name that is familiar to many Christians. Bonhoeffer was a Lutheran pastor who opposed Hitler. He taught others to be pastors in a clandestine church that they called the Confessing Church. When it became apparent to Bonhoeffer that the only way to stop the evil that Hitler perpetrated upon ethnic groups, he agreed to be a part of the plot to assassinate Hitler and form a new German government. The Bunker plot failed, and Hitler only suffered a partial loss of hearing. All those who were a part of the conspiracy were arrested, and Hitler himself ordered that they all be executed.

After being transferred from several prisons and concentration camps, Bonhoeffer was taken to the extermination camp at Flossenburg. On April 9, 1945, one month before Germany surrendered, he was hanged naked with six other resisters.

A decade later, a camp doctor who witnessed Bonhoeffer's hanging described the scene: "The prisoners ... were taken from their cells, and the verdicts of court martial read out to them. Through the half-open door in one room of the huts, I saw Pastor Bonhoeffer, before taking off his prison garb, kneeling on the floor praying fervently to his God. I was most deeply moved by the way this lovable man prayed, so devout and so certain that God heard his prayer. At the place of execution, he again said a prayer and then climbed the steps to the gallows, brave and composed. His death ensued in a few seconds. In the almost fifty years that I have worked as a doctor, I have hardly ever seen a man die so

We're On The Move Now!

entirely submissive to the will of God."

Dietrich Bonhoeffer's last words reflected that he knew he was a child of God. Bonhoeffer said, "This is the end — for me the beginning of life."

Amen.

Christmas 2

Ephesians 1:3-14

153
The Abounding Grace Of God

O Come, All Ye Faithful is a translation of a Latin hymn *Adeste Fidelis*. The original hymn, written in Latin, was composed by monks in the thirteenth century. The first two words *Adeste Fidelis*, means "come you faithful ones." The manuscript was left undiscovered until John Francis Wade located it in 1745. He then translated the hymn from Latin into English, as well as adding a few verses.

O Come, All Ye Faithful draws us into the Christmas story of the shepherds, as recorded in Luke's Gospel. In this beloved passage angels appear to shepherds, glorifying God because of the birth of the Savior, the Messiah, who lies in a manger in Bethlehem. After the angels leave, the shepherds decide to go to Bethlehem in order to find the Christ child. As the hymn recounts the event of that starry night, the shepherds may have said to each other, "Come, let's go to Bethlehem. Let's come and behold the king of angels." But, now, our beloved Christmas hymn invites all of God's faithful to come, including you and me.

O come, all ye faithful, joyful and triumphant!
O come ye, O come ye to Bethlehem;
Come and behold him
Born the King of Angels:
O come, let us adore Him,
Christ the Lord.

Our Lectionary reading this morning, Ephesians 1:3-14, is a hymn. The first century church sang many liturgical hymns during worship. Some of these hymns are reproduced in part and in their entirety. They were used by the writers of the gospels and epistles as a means of sharing a doctrinal truth. Remembering that most first century Christians were illiterate, by hearing a familiar hymn it would add clarity to the pulpit message.

Our hymn in Ephesians was sung as a baptismal liturgy. The message of the hymn is what does it mean to be baptized? What does it mean to have God forgive our sins and that we have now become a part of God's heavenly family? The hymn expresses the first-century church's liturgical doctrine on the meaning of baptism.

If we would walk through the hymn stanza by stanza the first century church's understanding of the sacrament of baptism will unfold before us:

- God through Jesus has blessed us with all the spiritual blessings found in heaven — in "heavenly places"
- Just as Jesus was "holy" and "blameless" — we who are baptized, by the grace of God, will be found holy and blameless
- We must live a life that is obedient unto God, that shows reverence by praising God
- God is no longer a "mystery" to us because Jesus has revealed God to us
- God now wants "to gather all things" — Jews and Gentiles alike — into one body — into one church
- The death and resurrection of Jesus was God's intervention in human history for redemption
- For this reason man was created to praise God
- Through the sacrament of baptism God has "sealed" within us God's blessings
- Baptism has made us the "adopted" sons of God — with baptism we shall receive our "inheritance" which are the heavenly blessings of God

The first-century doctrine of baptism pronounces that with baptism we have been forgiven of our sins, which means we have been adopted into God's family; that is, we are children of God. As a child of God we have received our inheritance from God. It is not a material inheritance, as preachers of the prosperity gospel would like us to believe, but it is a spiritual blessing of unlimited proportions. As a child of God, we are obedient and glorify his name.

Megachurch pastor Joel Osteen, with his spinning globe in lieu of a cross at this Lakewood Church in Houston, makes no apology for his personal financial gain from his 52,000 weekly attendees and his 700,000 email recipients, who believe that Osteen's obnoxious wealth can be theirs by obedience to the fraudulent scriptural mandates of the of the prosperity gospel. Osteen, who purchased a sports arena and transformed it into colosseum sanctuary, with the luxury of theater seats, defended his repugnant wealth with this remark, "I think people in my congregation would say, 'Wow! God has blessed Joel and Victoria!' I think the people I'm talking to would say that if God did it for me, he can do it for them."

Joel Osteen, who by his own admission is theologically uneducated, confesses that his only theological education came for editing his father's sermons for television. He will never acquiesce to the teaching of Dr. Andrew Purves, a professor at Pittsburgh Theological Seminary and a proponent of the theology of compassion, who once wrote, "There is a power for ministry in those who are themselves wounded, who have received the comfort of God, and who now minister to others in the strength of healing."

Osteen's comment reflects the theological illiteracy of populist preachers, who promote the prosperity of personal wealth over sacrificial discipleship. These preachers would presently include along with Joel Osteen, Joyce Meyer, Creflo Dollar, Kenneth Copeland, Bruce Wilkinson, Paula White, Benny Hinn, and T. D. Jakes. Previous preachers of financial wealth through a distorted gospel message, a message used for their own personal financial gain, would present the familiar names of Rex Hubbard, Oral Roberts, Norman Vincent Peale, and Robert Schuller.

It is a distorted gospel message, as Joel Osteen preaches to his worldwide congregation, come and share in my financial wealth, rather than, *let me come and share in your pain and suffering*. It is the perverted message that right thinking, or positive thinking, will bring you blessings from heaven a hundredfold; instead of presenting the message that right thinking is soul thinking that motivates a Christian "to suffer with."

In baptism, the blessings we receive from God will never be materialistic; they will always be spiritual. God realizes that flying first class, having a personally owned Lear jet, a mansion to reside in along with a summer home, and even something as ridiculous as Jim and Tammy Bakker's air-conditioned doghouse is not our inheritance. Those who abuse the gospel message want us to believe our blessings are materialistic, but authentic Christians realize our blessings will always be spiritual.

As we learn in the gospel of John, chapter 21, that after the resurrection, Jesus met with some of the disciples on the shore of the Sea of Galilee. Simon Peter decided to go fishing and he was joined Thomas, Nathanael, the sons of Zebedee, and two other unnamed disciples. Fishing all night, they caught nothing. Then Jesus, in the morning, instructed them to cast their net over the right of the boat. Suddenly they caught 153 large fish - so many fish that their net was about to break. There were so many huge fish they could hardly pull their net to shore.

In the Bible some numbers are sacred, and their meaning never changes throughout the scriptures. The study of these sacred numbers is called biblical numerology. The number 153 comes from number one, which means God; number five which means grace; and number three which represents the Trinity or the Godhead. The number 153 means the abundance of God's grace, the abundance of God's spiritual blessings. It is a spiritual abundance so large that no Christian will be in want. That is what it means in baptism when we become a child of God and an heir to God, in which we receive the overflowing spiritual blessings, not materialistic blessings, from God's grace. In thankfulness, we joyfully dedicate ourselves to follow God's teachings and engage ourselves in God's service.

Obedience begins with the study of God's word as recorded in the scriptures. We begin with the gospels to gain an understanding of how Jesus lived and how Jesus expected us to live our lives. The most important section of the gospels is Mathew, chapters five, six, and seven, which is the Sermon on the Mount. With this teaching Jesus outlined his systematic theology, which is an orderly and systematic presentation of his beliefs. We next focus on the epistles, the letters of Paul, Peter, and others. This teaches us how we are to live within the church. These letters emphasize the importance of community. As we move onto the Old Testament we will learn about the God of the covenant and deliverance.

In our quest to know God we attend worship for inspiration, but we attend Sunday school for a chance to learn and dialogue. We attend special education programs, like the traditional Wednesday evening dinner followed by a Bible study, in order to take advantage of another opportunity to learn. In addition to our private devotions we join a small group. This intimate group will allow unhindered dialogue, as well as always holding us accountable to our Christian lifestyle.

We are then ready to be obedient to the service of God. Again, the church presents for us a number of opportunities to become involved. Our Sunday school class and small group can also take on a service project. And as a Christian, as an individual, we can always see an opportunity to assist someone else. In doing these things we are living our baptism.

A Charlie Brown Christmas follows Charlie Brown as he fights the holiday's commercialism and searches for the true meaning of Christmas. In the show's final scene, Linus takes center stage at a play practice and recites Luke 2:8-14. Linus is alone on stage, highlighted by a single spotlight.

When Schulz proposed this, that famous scene was added to the special over the objections of the producer Lee Mendelson and director Bill Melendez. They believed that Peanuts creator Charles M. Schulz had crossed a line in wanting Linus to recite the Bible.

In an interview with *Huff Post*, Mendelson recalled their initial reaction to Schulz's proposal, which was actually an uncompromising demand on the part of Schulz. Mendelson recalled, "I said, 'Sparky, this is religion. It just doesn't go in a cartoon,'" Then Sparky, the nickname of Schulz, "looked at me very coldly and said, 'Bill, if we don't do it, who will? We can do it.'" Mendelson agreed. Schultz was right.

Schultz went on to say, as Mendelson recounted, "When Schulz said, 'You know, we're going to have Linus read from the Bible,' Bill and I looked at each other and said, 'Uh oh, that doesn't sound very good,' But then Schulz said, 'Look, if we're going to do this, we should talk about what Christmas is all about, not just do a cartoon with no particular point of view.'"

More than fifty years after it first aired in 1965, *A Charlie Brown Christmas* remains one of the most beloved television specials of the season among people of faith, primarily due to Linus bold recitation of the gospel message.

Let us live our baptism with a bold proclamation of the gospel message.

Amen.

Baptism of Our Lord

Acts 19:1-7

Tata Jesus Is Bangala!

"Tata Jesus Is Bangala!" declares the Reverend every Sunday at the end of his sermon. More and more, mistrusting his interpreters, he tries to speak for himself in Kikongo. He throws back his head and shouts these words in the sky, while the attendees sit scratching themselves in wonder. "Bangala" means something precious and dear. But the way he pronounces it, it means the poisonwood tree. So, he preaches, "Praise the Lord, hallelujah, my friends! For Jesus will make you itch like nobody's business."

This paragraph was written by Barbara Kingsolver in her novel *The Poisonwood Bible*, that was published in 1998. It is the story of the Price family who made a pilgrimage from Bethlehem, Georgia to the Belgian Congo as missionaries in 1959. Reverend Nathan Price, autocratic and self-righteous, was an old school missionary who firmly believed that the gospel of salvation coupled with Americanization was the only viable means to transform a tribal people into a civilized society. Aghast rather than respectful of their customs, not only was he unable to speak their language but he failed to comprehend the significance and beauty of an intricate social system that he could only view as barbaric.

As an uncompromising Baptist minister, Price held firm that salvation required baptism, and baptism necessitated being immersed. The only water suitable for the sacrament of repentance was the river. Repeatedly the villagers would flee rather than flock when summoned to the riverbank for baptism.

It took many months for Price to learn that several children had been devoured by crocodiles that lurked in those forbidden murky river waters. Inflexible, even with this discovery, he remained relentless in his pursuit to baptize converts in the hellish river. What well-meaning parent would place a son or daughter in such danger for any god; especially one when worshiped with joyful hallelujahs who could bring upon them an unforgiving rash?

Coinciding the gospel of Jesus Christ to diverse cultures is a perennial issue for the church. Thankfully, we have matured in recent decades with mainline Protestant denominations having learned to be respectful, recognizing that the traditions and customs of others can enlighten our own concept of the deity. Nevertheless, we must realize cultural misunderstanding of the personhood of Jesus began during the early stages of church growth.

Cultural and theological misunderstanding was a problem that plague the churches in Ephesus. Paul returned to Ephesus after his missionary journey to Corinth was completed. He remained in Ephesus for two years, which was his last residential ministry. When Paul arrived he discovered that there were Christians who were following John the Baptist. They were following the baptismal instructions of John the Baptist, which was a call for repentance. But they had not heard of the blessing that comes in being baptized in the name of Jesus, which is the gift of being baptized in the Holy Spirit.

William Barclay, who resided in Glasgow, Scotland, was born in 1907 and died in 1978, was a Scottish author, radio and television presenter, a Church of Scotland minister, and a Professor of Divinity and Biblical Criticism at the University of Glasgow. He wrote a popular set of Bible commentaries on the New Testament that has had millions and millions of readers. The seventeen-volume commentary was titled *The Daily Bible Study*.

In his volume on the book of Acts, and reviewing today's lectionary reading, Barclay interpreted our lesson as having two stages for baptism. The first stage was the preaching of John the Baptist, and his message was a "threat." John knew his preaching only pointed to the one who would come. This is the stage when we recognize our own "inadequacy and the fact that we are deserving of condemnation at the hand of God." The message of baptism from John was a call for "repentance."

The second stage came with Jesus who preached "good news." Jesus came with a message of "grace." It is a message of forgiveness. Our condemnation has been taken away. We also know that "closely linked with that stage is the time when we find that all our efforts to do better are strengthened by the work of the Holy Spirit, through whom we can do what we never could do on our own."

Barclay concluded with these words, "The incident shows us one great truth — that without the Holy Spirit there can be no such thing as a complete Christian."

This is why Paul was so astonished that the Christians he encountered in Ephesus did not know about being baptized in the Holy Spirit, and why Paul was so insistent that he laid his hands upon them so they may receive the baptism of the Holy Spirit. It was, for the Christians in Ephesus, a new Pentecost. It was a new Pentecost, for as the first Pentecost, under the pastoral oversight of Peter, the Christians now, under the pastoral oversight of Paul, "spoke in tongues and prophesized."

Recorded throughout the scriptures are the multiple blessings that come from receiving the Holy Spirit. Jesus taught, as recorded in John 14:15-17, "If you love me, keep my commandments. I will ask the Father to give you another helper, to be with you always. He is the Spirit of truth, whom the world cannot receive, because it neither sees him nor recognizes him. But you recognize him, because he lives with you and will be in you." In some translations "helper" is translated as "advocate." The Holy Spirit will speak on our behalf. The Holy Spirit will intervene on our behalf. Jesus also taught, as recorded in John 14:26, "But the helper, the Holy Spirit, whom the Father will send in my name, will teach you all things and remind you of everything that I have told you." With the Holy Spirit dwelling within us, we will continue to come to a fuller understanding of the teachings of Jesus.

Paul understood, in this same vein, that the Holy Spirit will strengthen us. Paul wrote in Romans 8:26, "In the same way the Spirit also joins to help in our weakness, because we do not know what to pray for as we should, but the Spirit himself intercedes for us with unspoken groanings." Paul also realized, as he wrote in 1 Corinthians 12:1-11, that the Holy Spirit brings us the gifts for ministry. Paul wrote, "Now there are varieties of gifts, but the same Spirit, and there are varieties of ministries, but the same Lord. There are varieties of results, but it is the same God who produces all the results in everyone. To each person has been given the ability to manifest the Spirit for the common good. To one has been given a message of wisdom by the Spirit; to another the ability to speak with knowledge according to the same Spirit; to another faith by the same Spirit; to another gifts of healing by that one Spirit; to another miraculous results; to another prophecy; to another the ability to distinguish between spirits; to another various kinds of languages; and to another the interpretation of languages. But one and the same Spirit produces all these results and gives what he wants to each person."

This is why our lesson this morning from Acts is so important for us today. We need the blessings and gifts, the intervention and support, that only the Holy Spirit can provide us. Those of us who now live in the twenty-first century. Those of us who now live more than two millennia from the first Pentecost, we are the ones, like the Christians at Ephesus who were only a few decades removed from the original day of

Baptism of the Lord

Pentecost, need an advocate who will guide us. We need a helper who will continue to enlighten us. We need the divine Spirit that will instill within us the gifts we need for a meaningful and productive ministry.

Our lesson also tells us that Paul laid his hands upon twelve individuals. If we would study biblical numerology the number twelve is significant. The symbolic meaning of certain numbers remains the same throughout the scriptures. The number one refers to God. The number three refers to the trinity. The number five refers to grace. The number six refers to Satan. The number forty refers to testing. The number seventy refers to judgment. The number twelve refers to leadership. We have the twelve tribes of Israel and we have the twelve apostles of Jesus.

When Paul laid his hands upon the twelve in the church in Ephesus, he was blessing the twelve leaders of the church. But today, we are all leaders. We may not be an ordained clergyperson, or an elder or a deacon, but we are leaders nonetheless. We are Christian leaders in our church, in our Sunday school class, in our evening study groups, in our homes, in our community, in our social circles and in our place of work. We exhibit Christian leadership wherever we may be. So, we need to know our Spiritual gifts and use them. We must call upon the advocate to intervene on our behalf. We must seek the insight provided to us by the helper.

Johannes Brahms, who was born in 1833 and died in 1897, was a German composer and pianist. His reputation and status as a composer are of such renown that he is sometimes grouped with Johann Sebastian Bach and Ludwig van Beethoven as one of the "Three Bs" of music. In his old age, Brahms told his friends that he was going to retire from composing music and enjoy the time left to him. But soon after that announcement a Brahms composition made its debut. When he was asked why he wrote a composition after saying he wasn't going to write anymore music Brahms replied, "I wasn't, but after a few days away from it, I was so happy at the thought of no more writing that the music came to me without effort."

With the blessing of the Holy Spirit we will be continually inspired. With the blessing of the Holy Spirit we will be continually motivated. With the blessing of the Holy Spirit we will be continually find our work for the Lord effortless.

Amen.

Epiphany 2

1 Corinthians 6:12-20

Your Body Is A Temple

Eva Longoria married Tony Parker, the point guard for the San Antonia Spurs, on July 6, 2007, in a civil ceremony at a Paris city hall. They had a Catholic wedding ceremony at the Saint-Germain l'Auxerrois Church in Paris on July 7, 2007. On November 17, 2010, Longoria filed for divorce from Parker in Los Angeles, citing "irreconcilable differences." Longoria told the media that she had discovered hundreds of text messages from another woman on her husband's phone. The other woman was Erin Barry, the wife of Brent Barry, Parker's former teammate. It was revealed that the Barrys' were also in the process of divorcing. Longoria and Parker were divorced in 2011.

After the divorce Longoria had a tattoo on her right wrist removed that had the Roman numeral "VII VII MMVII," which means "7-7-2007," which exhibited her wedding date with Tony Parker. She also had a tattoo on the back of her neck removed. This tattoo was the number "nine," in honor of the number on Parker's jersey that he wore while paying for the San Antonio Spurs.

In 2012 *People* magazine considered Eva Longoria, the former *Desperate Housewives* star, the woman who was most "beautiful at every age."

If one cannot remain faithful to the most beautiful woman of any age, then there must be something to a marital relationship beyond beauty and sex. A relationship is hollow absent of an emotional attachment. A relationship can only be sustained with meaningful conversation. A relationship will persevere only with genuine love and support. Prostitutes and fornication do not fit into this picture, as Paul tried to convince the Christians who resided in the church at Corinth.

The problem resided on two fronts. There was one relating to culture and one relating to theology.

The culture that prevailed was that Corinth was a Hellenized city. Hellenization began in the three hundred years before the writings of Paul, when Alexander the Great spread the Greek culture among the countries he conquered. The Greeks always looked down on the body.

They had a proverbial saying that went like this: "The body is a tomb." The Greek philosopher Epictetus said, "I am a poor soul shackled to a corpse." Epictetus was a stoic Greek philosopher who wrote during the same years that Paul wrote his letters.

In the city of Corinth the Greeks had a temple called Acrocorinth. At this temple, worship would consist of visiting temple prostitutes. The Greeks also had a great social club called Asclepius. It was located on the edge of the city with a swimming pool, dining facilities and a garden. Meat from the worship of idols was served at dinner. The club was a famous gathering place for the gentry, where prostitutes and fornication were common.

The Corinth Christians were living in this culture. Surrounded by lust, one of the seven deadly sins, their temptation to indulge in the cultural practices of the Greeks must have been great.

There was also a Christian movement that Paul strongly opposed, that was called gnosticism. Gnostics believed that man's body, like all material things, was the creation of an inferior deity. Only the soul, which is not material, was created by God and sacred. Therefore, the body, like all material things, was destined for destruction. This meant that the gnostics held to the belief that bodily functions possessed no importance for a man's spiritual life. This meant that sexual acts, such as fornication and visiting prostitutes, could not defile the human spirit. Only the spirit could inherit the kingdom of God.

Gnosticism comes from the Greek word *gnosis*, which means "knowledge." Gnosticism means "having knowledge." Gnosticism was a heretical movement within the church until the second century. This was when Irenaeus, Bishop of Lugdunum, located in Gaul, which is present day France, began to write against it.

The problems in the Corinth church were brought to Paul's attention by letters written to him from Chloe. There is very little that we know about Chloe in the Bible. Only one verse mentions her name, which is 1 Corinthians 1:11 which says, "My brothers and sisters, some from Chloe's household have informed me that there are quarrels among you." What we know from this verse is that Chloe was a Christian woman living in Corinth and that she was an acquaintance of the apostle Paul. Because Paul refers to her by her first name, Chloe, it is likely she was well known to the believers of that area, possibly a householder who held worship services in her home. The reports by Chloe were not idle gossip, but they were an attempt to get Paul's assistance in resolving problems within the church. In response to Chloe's request for assistance, we have our lectionary reading for this morning.

Paul, in his attempt to bring the Corinth church back into the obedience of his teaching when he visited there twice, had as his battle cry, "You are not your own; you were bought at a price. Therefore, honor God with your bodies."

Paul considered our bodies to be united with Christ. Throughout his writings we know that Paul offer refers to the fact that we are the body of Christ. So, if we unite our bodies with a prostitute, we defile the body of Christ. Paul writes, "Do you not know that your bodies are members of Christ himself? Shall I then take the members of Christ and unite them with a prostitute? Never! Do you not know that he who unites himself with a prostitute is one with her in body? For it is said, 'The two will become one flesh.'"

The question that comes to us is, "Have we defiled the body of Christ?" Have we defiled the body of Christ through our actions and behavior? We may not be fornicators, having remained faithful to our marital vows. We may never have visited a prostitute. We may never even have had the inclination to visit a prostitute, but does that mean we have never defiled the body of Christ? It is time for all of us to examine our Christian lifestyle!

We may not be fornicators. We may not have visited prostitutes. But does that mean we have never lusted? Does that mean we have never engaged in one of the seven deadly sins?

Evagrius Ponticus, also known as Evagrius the Solitary, was a Christian monk and ascetic who resided in a monastery in the Egyptian desert. Concerned with the temptations that besought people the most, in the year 375 he compiled a list of the eight terrible thoughts, also referred to as the eight evil temptations. The eight patterns of evil thought are gluttony, greed, sloth, sorrow, lust, anger, vainglory, and pride. The list was not to be one of condemnation; rather, it was to raise awareness to our most compelling temptations so that we would be self-disciplined enough to avert our attention from them. Almost two centuries later, in the year 590, Pope Gregory I, also known as Pope Gregory the Great, revisited the list and refined it to seven by combining two and adding two more of his own. Gregory's list is more commonly known as the seven deadly sins, which are: pride, envy, anger, sloth, greed, gluttony, and lust.

Now, some 1,400 years later, as we move into the twenty-first century, perhaps we ought to restore the list to eight. This time adding a temptation that had not appeared before but is appropriate for a technological society. The new temptation would be "fame." In *The New York Times* an article was printed on November 11, 2009, by Alessandra Stanley who wrote, "Fame has a spellbinding power in American society, the one thing that can trump wealth, talent, breeding, and even elected office. Reality shows and social websites like Facebook long ago knocked down barriers that kept ordinary people trapped in obscurity." For this reason Stanley wrote, "…some people take huge risks for the freedom to be someone else — a celebrity." She lifted up as examples the Salahis' who crashed a White House state dinner, the Heenes who pretended a child was trapped in a runaway balloon, and the Gosselins who showcased their eight children, all desiring to share the limelight of a reality television show.

Has your cell phone become an instrument of lust? It certainly seems that the cell phone has become an idol, something we worship as we are constantly checking it. And with our cell phone we do abuse others. We may not send bullying messages, but how often do we place a cell phone message that we have to check and answer this exact second, at the expense of the individual we are visiting with.

Rana Awdis wrote the book, *In Shock*, which was published in 2017. Just out of medical school she was a critical care physician when she encountered some serious medical problems resulting from her pregnancy. The focus of the book is how physicians are disconnected from the emotional needs of their patients. Something she was never aware of as a physician, but became acutely aware of as a patient.

Sadly, this was also true for her husband Randy. At the hospital she urged Randy to come immediately to her aid and support. She wrote, "Randy, who was an attorney at a law firm in the city, answered something about leaving as soon as he responded to the mythical 'one final email,' confirming to me that I had failed to convey the immediacy of my need." Randy was slow and long in coming. Several paragraphs later Awdis wrote, "To this day he insists it was without responding to the email, although I am less certain of that."

I need not belabor the point. We are all fornicators. We have all visited prostitutes. Perhaps not literally, but we have all violated the seven deadly sins. I know we have all violated the eighth deadly sin. How many of you have peaked at your cell phone during this worship service?

Paul did provide an insightful answer to Chloe. He wrote back to her saying that she must remined the Christians at Corinth that, "Do you not know that your bodies are temples of the Holy Spirit, who is in you, whom you have received from God? You are not your own; you were bought at a price. Therefore, honor God with your bodies."

Our bodies are the temple of the Holy Spirit. What we do with our bodies, our minds, our mouths, our actions, our behavior, directly reflect on our relationship to Jesus. Others will observe all of these. Depending on the temple we display to them, they will question or be assured of our genuineness in serving our Lord.

When running for the office of President of the United States, Jimmy Carter allowed himself to be interviewed by *Playboy* magazine. The now famous November 1976 publication almost cost him the election against presiding President Gerald Ford. He gave the controversial interview to Robert Sheer. In the interview Carter said, "I tell you that anyone who looks on a woman with lust has in his heart already committed adultery. I've looked on a lot of women with lust. I've committed adultery in my heart many times. This is something that God recognizes I will do — and I have done it — and God forgives me for it."

Let us live knowing our bodies our the "temple of the Holy Spirit."
Amen.

Epiphany 3

1 Corinthians 7:29-31

We're On The Move Now!

The Seven-Day Adventist denomination celebrated their 150-year anniversary in May 1994. Yet, they looked upon it as a failure, for their denomination was founded upon the principle of the immediate return of Jesus. Lisa Beardsley-Hardy, the denomination's director of education, said, "It's almost an embarrassment to be celebrating 150 years." Michael Ryan, a vice-president, said, "In one kind of way it really is a sad event."

Paul expected the immediate return of Jesus, and this influenced much of his writings. In fact, Paul expected Jesus to return — the Second Coming — the Parousia — in his lifetime. This concept of eschatology — the theology of the end times — guided all his theology. The word eschatology arises from the Greek *eschatos* meaning "last" and *-logy* meaning "the study of." Eschatology is the study of the end times.

Believing that Jesus would return in a few decades, perhaps in a few years, and maybe in a few weeks, Paul did not want anything to interfere with service and devotion to Jesus. Not understanding this, we have misinterpreted much of what Paul wrote regarding society.

Paul did not oppose marriage, but it was unnecessary for the short time we had left before the return of Christ. Yet, Paul understood, if you could not restrain your sexual impulses then it was acceptable to get married. This is also why Paul encouraged widows not to remarry. Regarding slaves — we never read where Paul condoned slavery, but with the immediate return of Christ it was best if slaves focused in their immediate station in life. Regarding slavery Paul wrote, "although if you can gain your freedom, do so." We also used his words in Romans as a mandate for blind obedience to the ruling authorities of our present age — to our government. Paul was not justifying an oppressive regime, what he was saying since Christ would return shortly, so let us not be disruptive for it will hinder our Christian witness. All of this points to a single fact for Paul the only thing that was important for a Christian was the proclamation of the salvation message in the name of Jesus.

We're On The Move Now!

There is also something that we misunderstood that caused and continues to cause countless social ills as we apply Paul's writings to today's society. Most of the time in the epistles Paul spoke as one whose authoritative writings were based on his revelation received on his Damascus road experience. But there were other times when Paul was just expressing his opinion, which is the case for today's lectionary reading. Paul introduced this section of our lectionary reading with the words "I mean." Paul was putting before the readers that what was to follow was his opinion, his personal thoughts, his personal ethical position, but it was not a direct command — it was not a direct mandate, from God.

How many lives have we ruined because we have failed to place Paul's writings in the proper eschatological context? How many lives have we ruined because we have taken Paul's opinion and made it into a legalistic mandate?

In 1844, a group of 50,000 followers expected the immediate return of Jesus. So strongly did they hold these beliefs, that many sold their possessions and others let their fields lie fallow. When Jesus did not return, the aftermath was called the Great Disappointment. Some, sadly, even committed suicide. In May of that year, the remaining followers organized themselves into a church. They called themselves Adventists for they expected the immediate return — the advent — of Jesus.

In our lectionary reading Paul wrote, "the appointed time has grown short." The time for the return of Jesus may have "grown short," but we are still waiting. But before we get too complacent let us remember the instruction of Jesus, as recorded in Matthew 24:37-39, when he said, "As it was in the days of Noah, so it will be at the coming of the Son of Man. For in the days before the flood, people were eating and drinking, marrying and giving in marriage, up to the day Noah entered the ark; and they knew nothing about what would happen until the flood came and took them all away. That is how it will be at the coming of the Son of Man."

Being a studious servant of Jesus should not depend on whether Jesus is returning this week, this month, this year, this decade, this century, or even this millennia. It should make no difference to us if it be one day or a thousand days. Our calling remains the same — to share the gospel message of salvation. But we should still be cautious, for we still live in the days of Noah.

John Wesley, the founder of Methodism in the mid-eighteenth century, was returning home after conducting an evening worship service when he was robbed. The robber took his money and the religious literature that he was carrying. As the robber began to dart off into the darkness of the night, Wesley called to him saying, "My friend, you may live to regret this sort of life. If you ever do, here's something to remember: 'The blood of Jesus Christ cleanses us from all sin!'"

Years later a distinguish businessman approached John Wesley. He introduced himself as the man who robbed Wesley that awful night. He had repented of his sins and was then an active Christian. The man said he owed his conversion to Wesley. To this remark he replied, "Oh no, my friend, not to me, but to the precious blood of Christ that cleanses us from all sin!"

We do not want to regret the sort of life we are living. And we certainly don't want to live a licentious life thinking we can make a death bed confession. Even though the sun is shining, the birds are singing and the air is cool, we must remember that the days for Christ return have "grown short." This is the since of immediacy that Paul wanted to instill in his readers. This is the sence of immediacy that Jesus wanted to instill in his hearers when he said "As it was in the days of Noah..."

Realizing Paul was offering us his opinion the days are long enough to be advocates for social justice. Realizing Paul was offering us his opinion the days are long enough so we can be activists for equality. Realizing Paul was offering us his opinion the days are long enough so we can be outspoken against oppression. But the days are too short for us not to be witnesses to the gospel message.

March 25, 1965. The Reverend Doctor Martin Luther King Jr. led a procession of 25,000 demonstrators into Montgomery, Alabama. Solemnly, the cortege passed the Jefferson Davis Hotel, which had a huge Rebel flag draped across its front. Quietly they stood at Confederate Square, where Negroes had been auctioned off in the days of servitude. Spontaneously, the multitude sang "Deep in my heart, I do believe; We have overcome — today." The cavalcade lurched forward, proceeding up Dexter Avenue, following the same path as Jefferson Davis' inaugural parade. These descendants of slaves freely strode to the portico of the capital; the place where Davis had taken his oath of office as President of the Confederate States. Governor George Corley Wallace refused to meet with the Freedom Marchers, nor would he receive their petition demanding the right to vote. The crowd milled in front of the statehouse, as the governor peered anxiously from behind his cracked office blinds.

Positioned below the governor's window, King stood on the flatbed of a trailer, readying himself to address the gathering. With television cameras focused on his round, intense face, and his body silhouetted against the setting sun, King intoned: "We are on the move now. The burning of our churches will not deter us. We are on the move now. The bombing of our homes will not dissuade us. We are on the move now. The beating and killing of our clergymen and young people will not divert us. We are on the move now. The arrest and release of known murderers will not discourage us. We are on the move now. Like an idea whose time has come, not even the marching of mighty armies can halt us. We are moving to the land of freedom."

"We are on the move now!" ought to be the battle cry of everyone. We rebuke any organization that promotes racism, sexism, and ageism. We denounce economic and social injustice. We deplore rules that dehumanize people. We condemn autocrats who are self-indulgent. We censure derogatory comments and gossip. We reprimand any individual that demeans or belittles another human being. We confront persons who are callous and insensitive. We sally forth allowing nothing — absolutely nothing — to stave off our protest."

To besiege the opposing forces in society requires single-minded obedience to the truth of the scriptures. Adhering to the sacred text, Christians must be willing to emulate the steadfast nature of Jesus. There came a time when Jesus of Nazareth realized he could no longer effectively continue his public ministry in Galilee; if the gospel message was to be heard, it must be proclaimed in Zion. The prophet was resolute in his decision, as Luke narrated, "When the days drew near for him to be received up, Jesus set his face to go to Jerusalem." (9:51) The Son of God chose to stand directly before the Sanhedrin, announcing that the year of Jubilee had come.

It was a lonely road that Jesus walked to Jerusalem; the disciples questioned him, Peter denied him, Thomas doubted, and one — Judas Iscariot — even betrayed him; the Sadducees challenged his theology, the Pharisees queried his motives, and the people called for Barabbas. Adamant, immutable, relentless, Jesus continued on his appointed course "to proclaim release to the captives and recovering of sight to the blind, to set at liberty those who are oppressed, to proclaim the acceptable year of the Lord" (Luke 4:18-19).

Andrew Jackson avowed, "One man with courage makes a majority." Empowered by the Holy Spirit, you can make a difference in the life of another person. You are expected to be an advocate for the powerless, a friend to the lonely, and offer hope to the forsaken. From this task you cannot waver.

In 1901, President William B. McKinley visited Niagara Falls. Encouraged by his entourage, he agreed to walk across the bridge connecting the United States with Canada. Great excitement prevailed, until he suddenly halted near the center of the bridge and returned home. McKinley explained that he did not want to be the first president to leave the boundaries of the United States while still in office.

In our calling to follow Christ we cannot go halfway, nor can we turn around. We must persevere, surmounting every obstacle placed in our path. Obliged to our Savior, we are undaunted in our mission.

Scolded and criticized, Abraham Lincoln still insisted on signing the Emancipation Proclamation. Defiant, the president answered his adversaries, "I am a slow walker, but I never walk back." We must go forward, if ever so slow. However small our steps, we must advance the cause of liberty and justice. Take your despondent brother by the hand, embrace your weeping sister and guide them to the promised land.

The journey is trying. Luke reported, "the people would not receive Jesus, because his face was set toward Jerusalem" (9:53). Even though he was ignored and shunned, the Messiah would not relinquish his commission. As futile as it may seem, we must never surrender to debauchery. Persecuted — we continue to chastise demagogues. Ridiculed — we never cease questioning the intemperate. Scorned — we still fervently announce the coming kingdom.

Martin Luther King Jr. stepped down off the trailer. The demonstration was over. It was time for everyone to return to Selma. The black participants, most unable to drive, were in need of transportation. White brothers and sisters from across the nation, Freedom Riders they were called, came to carry them home.

One volunteer was Viola Liuzzo, a mother of five, who traveled from Detroit to protest segregation. Unfamiliar with the roads, Mrs. Liuzzo was given a nineteen-year-old black guide. On her second trip from Selma a car followed behind her; soon there was a high-speed chase on Highway 80. Shots rang out in the night, her windshield shattered, and Viola Liuzzo died at the wheel of her car. Four members of the Ku Klux Klan were arrested for murder, but the district attorney refused to prosecute. President Lyndon Baines Johnson condemned the killing. Addressing the nation on television, the president said Mrs. Liuzzo "was murdered by enemies of justice, who for decades have used the rope and the gun, the tar and the feathers to terrorize their neighbors. They struck by night... for their purposes cannot stand the light."

The days are short as we are summoned to turn our face toward Jerusalem. The journey is perilous, for it ends at Golgotha.

Amen.

Epiphany 4

1 Corinthians 8:1-13

A Child Of God

Perry Noble of NewSpring Church, the worship leader of 32,000, the largest church in South Carolina with multiple campuses, caused a theological stir with his Christmas Eve sermon in 2016, proclaiming that the Ten Commandments were not commandments, but only "promises" since the word for "commandments" is not in the Hebrew lexicon. Having this epiphany, he wrote a revolutionary sermon in ten minutes transforming "you shalt not" to "you are free ..."

Reputable theologians challenged the irrefutable pastor regarding his exegesis. Though the Hebrew word used in the Torah can mean promises, it can also be interpreted as "declarations." It would seem "Thou shall not..." is hardly a promise but most certainly a declaration, which is a commandment. Noble later confessed there was a Hebrew word for "commandment," but stood by his sermon that Moses on Mount Sanai was given ten promises.

Since its conception, the church has been plagued by heretical teachings, which in the first five centuries required numerous ecumenical councils to establish orthodoxy. The heretical disease has persisted with each generation of pulpiters who misrepresented the gospel message to promote a singular credence unauthenticated by the established church.

Perhaps promises have a place at NewSpring, for a visitor is immediately informed that it is a church, but not like denominational churches. Rock bands, light shows, and vulgarity from the pulpit would substantiate that.

Noble is not the only Elmer Gantry among us. Joel Osteen admits he has no theological education and learned to preach by editing his father's sermons for television. This groomed him for preaching at Lakewood Church the soothing message of the prosperity gospel. Perhaps this is why his pulpit is centered before a turning globe of perpetual world blessings, replacing the harsh reality of the cross.

Rick Warren, of Saddleback Church, expounds a theology of life teaming with purpose; but, with his cornucopia of expositions on predestination, a purposeful life becomes null and void. *The Purpose*

Driven Life succeeded not for its theology but by an intensive marketing campaign prior to publication. Mark Driscoll, of Mars Hill Church, did even better as he hired a marketing firm to clandestinely purchase multiple copies of his book *Real Marriage* to propel it onto the bestselling list.

The growth of Saddleback was not birthed by Warren's fabricated theology. It arose from a young youth pastor who studied the demographics of California and located the fastest growing county, Orange, then the fastest growing neighborhood in that county, and there planted his church. Was it gospel growth or demographic growth?

Robert Schuler had the same *modus operandi* with the Crystal Cathedral. He may have exalted his humble origins of preaching at a drive-in theater, but it was located in the growing affluent white middle-class community of Garden Grove. Unfortunately, decades of white flight transformed the community to a poor catholic Latino neighborhood, and that majestic edifice of glass is now St. Callistus Roman Catholic Church.

Today we have megachurch pastors who are theological charlatans. Rick Warren seems to have twisted theology when he wrote we suffer "because God is developing within us the character of Christ," as opposed conventional theology that Christ suffered to be one with us. Yet, his charisma and business acumen, like most mega-church pastors, is able to fog heterodoxy.

Megachurches are great theatrical productions that foster a flimsy faith. Boasting nonconformity, they renounce the traditions provided by Christendom, thereby denying parishioners of the important faith sustaining components of liturgies, creeds, and hymns — heritage.

It is sad that Joyce Meyer can walk the corridors of these congregations, but doors are barred to the great theologians of our age, such as William Temple and Harry Emerson Fosdick.

Noble Perry published his book titled *Overwhelmed*, a pop-psychology blueprint to overcome stress. Yet he concludes with a very stressful plea, "One hundred thousand is on the way!" And so, we are given the measurement for pastoral success — numbers — not spirit.

By the way, Perry was removed from his pastorate for alcoholism and abuse of his staff members and his spouse. After seventeen years of marriage they divorced. But not to be undone, he started an internet church that in Anderson, South Carolina, the site for the original New-Spring Church. The new church has been called Second Chance Church, and in January 2019 it moved into a building in Anderson. What they are doing is taking advantage of someone who admires charisma. What they are doing is taking advantage of someone who is susceptible to hype. What they are doing is taking advantage of someone who will believe in their false promises. What they are doing, according to Paul, is taking advantage of someone who is weak in the Christian faith.

This problem, which engulfs us today, is the same problem that confronted Paul in the mid-first century. It is pastors — it is Christians who put themselves first. It is Christians who think they are more knowledgeable, and allowing them to dictate to others how to believe. It is Christians who think *their* way is the *only* way. It is Christians who think their understanding of the scriptures is the only understanding one can have.

For us today it is megachurch pastors who tell us that putting money in their pocket will bring us multiple blessings. For Paul it was puffed up Christians who would eat meat offered to idols, telling weaker Christians of maturity in the faith that they are foolish for abstaining. For us today is a denominational confrontation over believers' adult baptism as opposed to infant baptism. For Paul it was audacity versus humility. For us today it is whether Holy Communion is "transubstantiation" or "consubstantiation." For Paul it was a matter of foregoing one's stubbornness to accommodate another. For Paul love was to take precedence over self-righteousness.

But the argument continues. Who is right?

The word "transubstantiation" derives from Latin — *trans* which means "across," and *substania* which means "substance." The term is employed in Roman Catholic theology to denote the idea that during the ceremony of the Mass the bread and wine are changed in substance into the flesh and blood of Christ, even though the elements appear to remain the same. This doctrine has no basis in scripture. There are traces of this dogma in some of the post-apostolic writings. It was adopted by the fourth Lateran Council, which convened in 1215. It was formalized at the Council of Trent, which was held from 1545 to 1563. The doctrine was reaffirmed at the Second Vatican Council, which was held from 1962 to 1965.

"Consubstantiation" was derived by Martin Luther, the founder in the sixteenth century of the Protestant Reformation. It is a term commonly applied to the Lutheran, and presently most Protestant denominations, to the communion supper. The idea is that in the communion the body and blood of Christ, the bread and wine, coexist in union with each other. Luther illustrated this by the analogy of the iron put into the fire whereby both fire and iron are united, yet each continues unchanged.

For Paul it was not who was most right, but who is most loving. For Paul it was not to be exclusive in one's doctrine, but to be inclusive. For Paul it was not to be belligerent, but it was to be conciliatory.

In our lectionary reading for today Paul wrote, "Be careful, however, that the exercise of your rights does not become a stumbling block to the weak." Corinth was a Roman city where the worship of idols was prevalent. The meat that was sacrificed to those idols would often be served at a home, as a tribute the idol that it was sacrificed for. Some of the other meat was sold in the marketplace. Some Christians — the "mature" Christians, the "knowledgeable" Christians — had no problem eating this meat. They knew that eating this meat would not have any influence on their Christian faith. They knew that this meat had no meaning to it. But "weaker" Christians, those who were new to the faith, were afraid that by eating the meat offered to idols would cause them to go back to pagan worship. Paul inquired of the "knowledgeable" Christians, why be a "stumbling" block to those who are new to the faith? Instead of being audacious, be humble. Instead of lording over someone, be a mentor.

It is a challenge for us to avoid being haughty, self-righteous, boisterous, exclusive.

It is a call for us to be inclusive, humble, accepting, loving.

One day Archbishop Fulton J. Sheen was dining alone in the Statler Hotel in Boston. Looking up from his meal he saw a shoeshine boy in dirty tattered clothes. When the headwaiter spotted the youngster, he was immediately ushered out of the building. Sheen, unable to finish his meal, left the restaurant in search of the lad. Sheen soon found the youngster and in the resulting conversation discovered the boy was expelled from his Catholic school for repeated acts of misbehavior. The Archbishop promised to get the boy back into school, while the boy protested that his expulsion was final. No one, the boy asserted, would be able to convince the Mother Superior to open the doors once more for a disobedient student.

Archbishop Sheen visited the Mother Superior and shared this with her: "I know of three boys who were thrown out of religious schools: one because he was constantly drawing pictures during geography class; another because he was fond of fighting; and the third because he kept revolutionary books hidden under his mattress. No one knows the valedictorians of those classes, but the first boy was Hitler, the second Mussolini, and the third Stalin. I am sure that if the superiors of those schools had given those boys another chance, they might have turned out differently in the world. Maybe this boy will prove himself worthy if you take him back." Unable to dispute the wisdom of Fulton Sheen, the Mother Superior reinstated the boy. Upon graduation, the young man accepted the calling to be a missionary among the Eskimos.

Every human being is a child of God, whom we must appreciate and admire. Each man, woman and child we encounter is to be treated with dignity and respect. At no time are we to turn away any individual because of that person's sex, age, race, social status, personality idiosyncrasies, or physical condition. Our guiding principle is to accept everyone as a friend.

Amen.

Epiphany 5

1 Corinthians 9:16-23

Here I Am, Lord

Dan Schutte was a 31-year-old Jesuit studying theology in Berkeley, California, when one of his friends asked him to write a song for an upcoming diaconate ordination mass. The request came on Wednesday, and the ordination service was on Saturday. On top of the short notice, Schutte had been suffering from the flu for several days. He sat at his desk with his guitar and a blank sheet of staff paper in front of him, praying, "God, if I'm going to do this for my friend, you're going to have to help me."

Schutte said he often used scripture as the basis of his songs, so as he thought about the idea of vocation for the ordination mass. He turned to the stories of the prophets, like Jeremiah, who asked God to give him the right words to say. "In all those stories, all of those people God was calling to be prophets have expressed in one way or another their humanness or their self-doubt," Schutte said. Because of the self-doubt that was often expressed by the prophets, Schutte changed the biblical passage from one of confidence "Here I am, Lord; here I stand, Lord" to the self-doubting final version: "Here I am, Lord; is it I, Lord?"

Schutte sketched out "Here I Am, Lord" over the course of two days. On Friday evening, he walked to his friend's house to deliver the song, pencil in hand, scribbling edits along the way.

When Schutte receives letters on how the song has helped an individual on his or her spiritual journey, he expresses his feelings with these words, "There's a whole constellation of feelings that surround it for me." "I feel so grateful that God seems to have chosen that song to accompany people through so many moments of their life.... I didn't plan that. I didn't know that the song was going to be special. I'm very aware that God is doing something beyond me when I get those letters from people.... It's also very humbling because it's something way, way far beyond what I can do."

What makes the hymn so powerful and inspiring is the change in point of view that the singer makes between the stanzas and the refrain.

The stanzas speak from the perspective of God in the first person singular, while the refrain, though remaining in first person, is from the perspective of the singers of the hymn offering their lives to God.

Each stanza reflects a paradox. The powerful God, creator of "sea and sky," "snow and rain" and "wind and flame" is also the God who hears the "people cry," bears the "people's pain" and "tend the poor and lame."

This is a hymn of transformation. God transforms the darkness into light in stanza one, melts "hearts of stone" with love in stanza two and nourishes the "poor and lame" with the "finest bread" — a clear Eucharistic reference.

Each stanza ends with the question, "Whom shall I send?" The refrain immediately offers the response, "Here I am, Lord."

The beautiful lyrics can be found online. Please look them up and read through them.

How many of us can say, "Here I am Lord, Is it I Lord?" How many of us can say, "I have heard you calling in the night." Most importantly, how many of us can say, "I will go Lord." The Lord is not offering us an invitation. What we have is a command to serve him. What we have is a mandate to preach the gospel message to all individuals.

William Barclay, who was born in 1907 and died in 1978 in Glasgow, Scotland, was a Scottish author, radio and television presenter, a Church of Scotland minister, and a Professor of Divinity and Biblical Criticism at the University of Glasgow. He wrote a popular set of Bible commentaries on the New Testament that has had millions and millions of readers. The seventeen-volume commentary was titled *The Daily Bible Study*.

In his volume on *The Letters to the Corinthians*, and reviewing today's lectionary reading, Barclay interpreted our lesson as having four teaching points. First, Paul considered it a "privilege." He did not proclaim the gospel message for money, but he did because it was a privilege to serve the Lord. Second, Paul regarded it as his "duty." Paul did not choose his work for the Lord, but it chose him. Third, Paul knew that every day he received a "great reward." Paul had the satisfaction of bringing the gospel message to all who would receive it. Fourth, Paul spoke of his "method of ministry." Paul would be accommodating of the socio-religious positions of others.

How many of us can give an affirmative answer to these four teaching points, as presented by the Reverend Doctor William Barclay? Do we consider it a "privilege" to serve the Lord? Are we willing to serve the

Lord absent of financial compensation? Do we consider it our "duty" to serve the Lord? Are we willing to serve the Lord because we have had a conversion experience? Do we consider it a "great reward" to serve the Lord? Are we willing to serve the Lord because we know we are enriching the spiritual lives of others? Do we consider our "method of ministry" when we serve the Lord? Are we willing to surrender the 'isms' of society to see everyone as our equal? To serve the Lord is a "privilege," it is a "duty," it does provide a sense of "great satisfaction."

Paul, in his letter, is addressing being a witness for the Lord. The willingness to share the gospel message of salvation. And sharing the message comes only with the desire to seek out those who need to hear the message. But we find ourselves making excuses not to witness. I don't know what to say. I can't answer the hard questions. Everyone I know is a Christian.

But, these are, just excuses. They are self-justifications not to witness. They are attempts to rationalize our hesitancies. I know there are societal limitations on where we can speak about our Christian faith. But if we take seriously the concept that it is a privilege, a duty and an activity of great spiritual reward, then we would fine opportunities. In fact, if we were really sincere and dedicated, we would not have to look for opportunities, we would see them surrounding us everywhere.

On October 14, 1912, Theodore Roosevelt left the Milwaukee hotel where he rested that night. As he walked out the door, striding to the waiting automobile that would take him to the convention hall where he would address the Progressive Party, an assassin stepped out of the crowd and shot the former president. The bullet went through Roosevelt's overcoat, spectacle case, and folded manuscript; it fractured his fourth rib, and lodged near his right lung. Stunned by the impact, Roosevelt fell backwards to the ground, coughed several times, then stood up, determined to walk to the awaiting car. Ignoring the protests that he should seek immediate hospital care, Roosevelt rebukes his aids saying, "I will deliver the speech or die, one or the other." He then journeyed to his appointed place.

Standing at the podium in the convention hall, looking out over the people massed in the grand auditorium, Roosevelt began his oration with these words: "Friends, I shall ask you to be as quiet as possible. I don't know if you fully understand that I have just been shot; but it takes more than that to kill a Bull Moose." Roosevelt finished his speech, then sought treatment for his wound fifty minutes after the assassination attempt.

Do we have such determination when it comes to sharing the gospel message? Do we have the attitude that nothing will stop us? Do we have the attitude that no obstacle is to great? Do we have the attitude that this is our uncompromising calling?

Paul's attitude was that nothing will stop him from proclaiming the good news! Paul's attitude was that no obstacle will stop him from offering the message of salvation! Paul's attitude was that he would remain steadfast in his call to be an apostle — an ambassador — for the Lord!

In our lectionary reading Paul wrote, "I do it all for the sake of the gospel, so I may share in its blessings."

Amen.

Transfiguration of the Lord

Mark 9:2-9

Into The Valley Of Despair

There is an important flow of events in our lectionary reading this morning. A flow of events that each individual sitting in the pews before me must be willing to accept as the flow of events in your own lives, as you live the Christian life. It begins with the solitude of a retreat, that is focused on prayer. It moves to a revelation that comes with the indwelling of the Holy Spirit. It ends with what is really a new beginning, going forth in a ministry to others.

Let us begin where our lectionary reading begins. Our lesson reads; "After six days Jesus took Peter, James, and John with him and led them up a high mountain, where they were all alone." There are a number of interesting biblical motifs in this passage of scripture. Jesus went up to a "high mountain." The Bible always depicts that going up to a high mountain as a time and a place for spiritual solitude. It is a time to renew your faith. It is a time to once again encounter God.

When I was younger – much younger – I used to go camping on the weekends. This for me was a high mountain experience. In the solitude of the woods it seemed as if the world had stopped. It was quiet. It was peaceful. It was relaxing. It was refreshing.

Having surrendered my ambition to go camping I have found new high mountains to climb for solitude. I often go to the church sanctuary and sit quietly, surrounded by those beautiful stained-glass windows, focused on the altar cross before me. I often go to a coffee shop. Although there are people there with a chatter of conversation; somehow, just sitting in an easy chair with a cup of coffee, surrounded by people yet still alone, is for me a time of renewal.

So, the question is now, "Where is your high mountain?" Where do you go for spiritual renewal? One of the things I enjoyed about being a minister, until I had to leave the profession because of my health, was the joy of living a hundred different lives. I would visit all of my parishioners at home, and those I could at work. One thing I discovered is how many different high mountains there are. There is a high mountain for every unique personality.

We're On The Move Now!

Some, like me, found it in camping. Others had weekend homes. Some went to the beach. Others took their boat out onto the lake. Some found it working on a hobby, such as woodworking. Other just sat in a comfortable chair, reading a book. But for each it was a time for renewal and refreshment.

So, the question again is, "Where is your high mountain?"

Jesus went up onto the high mountain to pray. There is no disputing the fact that prayer is a central theme in the Bible. In fact, it would be near impossible to find a biblical character who did not pray.

Prayer is so important it is the only thing that the disciples asked to be taught. In Luke's gospel we read where the disciples said to Jesus, "Lord, teach us to pray, just as John taught his disciples." Then the scriptures read, "Jesus said to them, 'When you pray, say: 'Father, hallowed be your name...'" Jesus taught them the prayer we say each Sunday in worship.

If Jesus prayed, that means we should pray.

Many of you, like myself, have morning devotions. Many of you, like myself, have a prayer list. But I wonder how many of you have run into my same problem – once you put someone or something on your prayer list, how to you remove them without guilt? I solved that by ripping my prayer list up on Saturday, and writing a new one on Sunday morning. I rationalized that if something was still important enough, I would remember it, and I would carry it over from Saturday morning to Sunday morning.

How many of you, like me, have a prayer list that looks like a letter to Santa Claus? It is just one "give me" after another. How many of you can't distinguish your prayer list from the shopping list you make out for the grocery store? This, of course, is not good. There are blessings which we must be thankful for.

I would like to share with you how I solved this problem of a "give me" prayer list. I make sure that a number of items on my prayer list have a plus sign next to them. A plus sign means those are a blessing. I make sure that my prayer list is not just a "give me," but it is also a "thank you."

So, the question now becomes, what does your prayer list look like? Does your prayer list look like a letter to Santa Claus, or does it look like a spiritual letter to our Lord and Savior?

When Jesus was on the high mountain in prayer, he had a revelation, or as the scriptures report he was "transfigured." Our lesson reads, "His clothes became dazzling white, whiter than anyone in the world could

Transfiguration of the Lord

bleach them." This is much the same as when Moses was on top of Mount Sinai and received the revelation of the Ten Commandments, he was transfigured. The power of the indwelling of the Holy Spirit made them brilliantly white, that is to say, it made them brilliantly "pure."

This revelation for Jesus was a revelation of reassurance. For God, his heavenly Father, our heavenly Father, spoke, "This is my Son, whom I love." This was an important message for Jesus to hear, because he would soon be facing the trauma of his trial before Pilate and his execution on the hill of Golgotha.

We are all confronting the hill of Golgotha. It does not mean we will hang on a cross, executed for our Christian beliefs. But that does not mean we are still not persecuted for our Christian beliefs. As our society becomes increasing more secular, Christianity is falling into disfavor. As more and more people are calling themselves spiritual, or just religious, but not Christian, not a part of the church, we who do call ourselves Christian, and we who do affirm our membership in the local church, are rapidly becoming a persecuted minority. So yes, we are climbing Golgotha's hill.

But there are other Golgotha's in our lives. There are many other hills of trauma that we are climbing. There is illness. There are marital problems. There is estrangement from our children. There is insecurity about our employment. There are concerns about money. As we live, we are constantly in the shadow of Golgotha. The problem of life is that we all live under the dark could of Golgotha.

This is why it is so important for us to hear from our heavenly parent, "You are my child, whom I love."

Jesus then came down off the mountain into the valley of despair. Into the valley of the hurts and sorrows of life. The valley where prayer has prepared him to minister. The valley he must walk on his journey to Golgotha. Our lesson reads, "As they were coming down the mountain, Jesus gave them orders not to tell anyone what they had seen until the Son of Man had risen from the dead."

It is like in my solitude of camping. I had to leave the woods. I had to once again enter the busyness of the world.

I have an water color painting in the dining room of my home, by an artist whose name I do not know. From a distance, sitting in the living room, it is clear that I am looking at painting of a pond surrounded by trees. But seated close to the painting in my dining room, the colors all blend together into a mosaic, and no pond or trees can be seen, only a brilliant mixing of colors. To this day I remain baffled as to how the artist accomplished this.

The painting for me has a spiritual message. Up close life can be so busy, so hectic, and so full of problems and uncertainties that everything just blends together. It is only when we go on a spiritual retreat, it is only when we get some distance, can we see things clearly. It is only then that we can journey into the valley of despair, ministering as God has called us to do. The Christian challenge is that we have got to come down off the mountain top and find our place in the valley. To find our place where we are called to minister unto others.

Each of us has a gift for ministry. It is our Christian obligation to use it. The gifts of ministry are not confined to Paul's list of spiritual gifts. The spiritual gifts are so much broader and encompassing than that. No one should feel left out of the call to Christian service. No one should feel that they have nothing to contribute to the ministry of the church.

I consider my gift to be spiritual guidance. I have Asperger's, which is on the autism spectrum. This means interpersonal relationships are very cumbersome for me. This means I spend almost all of my time alone, in isolation really. But my gift has evolved into reading, writing, and researching. I use reading, writing, and researching to compose articles, sermons, books, public speeches, and edit the sermons and speeches of others who do mingle with the public.

What is your spiritual gift? Do you even know what your spiritual gift is? And if you know what your spiritual gift is, do you use it?

Your spiritual gift does not have to be speaking in tongues, healing, or prophecy. Believe it or not, your spiritual gift could be coaching little league baseball with a kind and teachable approach. Believe it or not, your spiritual gift could be arranging flowers for special occasions. Believe it or not, your spiritual gift could be could be lawn maintenance. Believe it or not, your spiritual gift is anything that you can do well that benefits someone else.

What has our lectionary reading taught us this morning? It means we are to go on a spiritual retreat. It means that while we are on the mountain top, we will be blessed with the indwelling of the Holy Spirit. It means we are to come down off the mountain into the valley of despair, where we will use our spiritual gifts to minister unto others.

Amen.